OPPORTUNITIES

in

Landscape Architecture, Botanical Gardens, and Arboreta Careers

REVISED EDITION

BLYTHE CAMENSON

New York   Chicago   San Francisco   Lisbon   London   Madrid   Mexico City
Milan   New Delhi   San Juan   Seoul   Singapore   Sydney   Toronto

Library of Congress Cataloging-in-Publication Data

Camenson, Blythe.
    Opportunities in landscape architecture, botanical gardens, and arboreta careers /
    Blythe Camenson. —Rev. ed.
        p.   cm.
    Includes bibliographical references (p.   ).
    ISBN 0-07-147608-3 (alk. paper)
        1. Landscape architecture—Vocational guidance—United States.   2. Botanical
    gardens—Vocational guidance—United States.   3. Arboretums—Vocational
    guidance—United States.   I. Title.

    SB469.384 C35   2007
    712.023—dc22   2006028900

1 2 3 4 5 6 7 8 9 10 11 12 13 14 15 16 17 18 19   DOC/DOC   0 9 8 7

ISBN-13: 978-0-07-147608-9
ISBN-10:   0-07-147608-3

Interior design by Rattray Design

McGraw-Hill books are available at special quantity discounts to use as premiums and
sales promotions, or for use in corporate training programs. For more information, please
write to the Director of Special Sales, Professional Publishing, McGraw-Hill, Two Penn
Plaza, New York, NY 10121-2298. Or contact your local bookstore.

This book is printed on acid-free paper.

CONTENTS

PART ONE: LANDSCAPE ARCHITECTURE

Extension Service. Canadian agricultural services. Job outlook for landscape design and maintenance.

PART TWO: BOTANICAL GARDENS AND ARBORETA

PREFACE

NORTH AMERICA IS filled with beautiful greenery, from the meticulously manicured lawns of a suburban neighborhood and the beautifully planned landscaping of an industrial park to botanical gardens, arboreta, city and national parks, and forests. To design and maintain these areas, a growing number of residential, commercial, and government clients rely on the services of a wide range of horticultural, landscape, forestry, and conservation specialists.

These professionals have the task of planning and caring for all kinds of land areas, paying attention to conservation and the impact on the environment as well as aesthetics. In some settings, they also have the opportunity to conduct research, seeking out and identifying plant forms, mapping and labeling them, and studying their characteristics and how they respond to their surroundings.

Those who are interested in and concerned about these issues can choose from many satisfying careers. As you read through this book, you'll learn about two broad categories that will introduce you to these careers. In Part One we look primarily at landscape architecture, the design of outside areas that are beautiful, functional, and compatible with the natural environment. We also investigate related professions—urban and regional planning, forestry and conservation, historic landscape preservation, landscape design and maintenance—and consider the wide variety of job responsibilities and the wide range of settings in which these professionals find work.

Part Two highlights the many careers available to those working in the specific settings of botanical gardens and arboreta, parks that are open to students and research scientists as well as the general public. Horticultural collections curators, propagators, educators, arborists, and a host of other professionals find satisfying work in these research-based settings.

Each field and setting carries with it different levels of responsibility and commitment. To identify occupations that will match your expectations, you need to know what each job entails.

The two parts of this book focus on the various work settings, the different job titles and duties, the necessary training, the salary you can expect to earn, and the job outlook.

Resources are also provided for you to find even more information. Professional associations and a variety of organizations maintain websites and publish newsletters and books to help you with your career choices. A suggested reading list of books and magazines in the various career fields is also provided.

In addition, professionals working in the different fields have contributed firsthand accounts to tell you what the work is really like. Their comments will help you to pinpoint the careers that might interest you and eliminate those that would clearly be the wrong choice. What better way to learn about a career than from someone already long involved in it?

Acknowledgments

The author would like to thank the following professionals for providing information about their work:

Jim Bauml, Senior Biologist
Anne Brennan, Student Intern
Kent Brinkley, Landscape Architect/Garden Historian
Rick Darke, Curator of Plants
Cliff Davidson, Urban and Regional Planner
Susan Farrington, Horticulturist
Stuart Felberg, State Trooper, Fish and Wildlife Division
Mark T. Folwell, Forester
Wesley Greene, Landscape Supervisor
Susan Kelley, Curatorial Associate
Kyle J. Lyssy, Landscape Designer

Thomas P. Mishler, Landscape Architect/Arboretum
   Director
Chris Strand, Outreach Horticulturist
Larry Walker, Range Conservationist
Matthew I. Zehnder, Landscape Architect

The author also wishes to thank Josephine Scanlon for her assistance with this revision.

PART ONE

Landscape Architecture

1

A CAREER IN LANDSCAPE ARCHITECTURE

EVERYONE ENJOYS ATTRACTIVELY designed residential areas, public parks, college campuses, shopping centers, golf courses, parkways, and industrial parks. These spaces are designed by landscape architects, whose goal is to combine function with beauty in a way that is compatible with the natural environment. Designs include planning the locations of buildings, roads, and walkways, as well as the arrangement of flowers, shrubs, and trees.

Historic preservation and natural resource conservation and reclamation are other important objectives that landscape architects address. They are hired by many types of organizations, from real estate development firms starting new projects to municipalities constructing airports or parks.

The American Society of Landscape Architects offers the following definition of the profession:

Landscape architecture as a profession applies artistic and scientific principles to the research, planning, design, and management of both natural and built environments. Practitioners apply creative and technical skills and scientific, cultural, and political knowledge in the planned arrangement of natural and constructed elements on the land with a concern for the stewardship and conservation of natural, constructed, and human resources. The resulting environments shall serve useful, aesthetic, safe, and enjoyable purposes.

History of Landscape Architecture

Frederick Law Olmsted is considered the father of U.S. landscape architecture. In 1858 he initiated a project—Central Park in New York City—that later redefined the industrial city. Historians credit the innovations of Central Park as having a tremendous evolutionary impact on park design, urban open space, parkways, pedestrian pathways, and transportation systems. Many believe that Olmsted addressed and influenced the core of what is good in American urbanism today.

Of course, Olmsted was not the first landscape architect, but his intense social commitment led him to focus on landscape architecture as the best way to solve so many of the urban problems of the mid-1800s. He was succeeded by others who applied and improved on his innovations. The historical development of landscape architecture follows in many ways the rapid growth of the United States during the last half of the nineteenth century and through all of the twentieth century.

Landscape architects became the leaders in social reform and in making our cities livable. They were the ones who offered plans for new towns and pointed out the need for parks and open space in our cities and suburbs. They also played a leadership role in writing and passing the legislation for the National Forest Act of 1898 and the National Parks Act of 1916, which established a world precedent for the preservation and management of natural resources.

Landscape Defined

To understand fully what the profession of landscape architecture entails, we first must consider a definition of *landscape*.

Landscape has been broadly defined as the entire outdoor environment in both cities and rural areas. On a small scale, this includes paving, fencing, and the detailing and planting of open spaces in cities and towns and around buildings. On a larger scale, landscape also takes into account the bigger problems of conservation and coastal and countryside management. In between these two extremes comes the full range of design and layout for recreation and industry, in both the private and public sectors.

Duties of the Landscape Architect

The goal of landscape architects is to solve problems concerning relationships between natural and built environments, which they accomplish by working on projects from the site design of a single building to large-scale developments with significant environmental impact.

Landscape architects also work on projects that conserve and protect natural resources. These projects may involve forest and wilderness areas, coastal areas, or the restoration of misused lands. Some conduct preservation and renovation planning to initiate design studies of historic and cultural resources for national, regional, and local historic sites and areas. (See Chapter 5 for more information on historic preservation.)

For the purposes of landscape preservation, development, and enhancement, landscape architecture may include the following tasks and considerations:

1. **Investigation, selection, and allocation of land and water resources for appropriate use.** Landscape architects are often involved in the development of a site from its conception, working with architects, engineers, scientists, and other professionals to determine the best arrangement of roads and buildings and the best way to conserve or restore natural resources.

2. **Feasibility studies.** In planning a site, landscape architects first consider the nature and purpose of the project and the available funds. They analyze the natural elements of the site, such as the climate, soil, slope of the land, drainage, and vegetation. They observe where sunlight falls at different times of the day and examine the site from various angles. They assess the effects of existing buildings, roads, walkways, and utilities on the project.

3. **Creation of graphic and written criteria to govern the planning and design of land construction programs.** Once feasibility decisions are made, landscape architects create detailed plans indicating new topography, vegetation, walkways, and landscape amenities. To account for the needs of the client as well as the conditions at the site, they may have to make many changes before a final design is approved. They must also take into account any local, state, or federal regulations, such as those protecting wetlands or historic resources. Once the design is complete, they prepare a proposal that includes detailed plans of the site, including written reports, sketches, models, photographs, land-use studies, and cost

estimates, which is submitted for approval by the client and by regulatory agencies.

Computer-aided design (CAD) has become an essential tool in preparing designs. Many landscape architects also use video simulation to help clients envision the proposed ideas and plans. For large-scale site planning, they also employ geographic information systems technology, such as a computer mapping system.

4. **Preparation, review, and analysis of master plans for land use and development.** These plans show the client the landscape architect's vision for the site. Once the plans are drawn, they are reviewed by the client and any governmental agencies involved in the project to ensure that they meet all environmental and regulatory requirements.

5. **Production of overall site plans, landscape grading, construction details, and plans for landscape drainage, irrigation, and planting.** If these plans are approved, landscape architects prepare working drawings that show all existing and proposed features. They also outline in detail the methods of construction, draw up a list of necessary materials, and prepare specifications, cost estimates, and reports for land development.

6. **Field observation and inspection of land area construction, restoration, and maintenance.** Although many landscape architects will supervise the installation of their design, some are also involved in the actual construction of the site; however, this is usually done by the developer or landscape contractor.

Specializations

Some landscape architects work on a wide variety of projects. Others specialize in a particular area, such as residential development, historic landscape restoration, waterfront improvement projects, parks and playgrounds, or shopping centers. Still others work in regional planning and resource management; feasibility, environmental impact, and cost studies; or site construction. Some landscape architects work in academic environments, teaching and conducting research.

Although most will do at least some residential work, few limit their practice to landscape design for individual home owners. The reason is because most residential design jobs are too small to provide suitable income compared with larger commercial or multi-unit residential projects. Some nurseries offer residential landscape design services, but these services often are performed by lesser-qualified landscape designers or others with training and experience in related areas.

Landscape architects who work for government agencies will do similar work at national parks, government buildings, and at other government-owned facilities. In addition, they may prepare environmental impact statements and studies on environmental issues such as public land-use planning.

Collaborative Effort

To deal with all these tasks involves a partnership of professionals skilled in a variety of areas: architects, engineers, town planners, surveyors, ecologists, foresters, and a whole range of other land-management professionals. While each of these focuses on solving problems within clearly defined limits, the landscape architect functions as a coordinator of sorts, collaborating with other specialists on interdisciplinary teams to solve environmental problems. In addition to understanding the roles of the various team members, the landscape architect has to anticipate problems and offer design solutions that consider new construction within a complicated and crowded landscape.

Working Conditions

Most landscape architects spend the bulk of their time in offices creating plans and designs, preparing models and cost estimates, doing research, and attending meetings. The rest of their time is spent at the project site. During the planning and design stage, they visit and analyze the site to verify that the design can be incorporated into the landscape. When the plans and specifications are completed, they may spend additional time on the site observing or supervising the construction.

Most landscape architects work regular hours, although overtime may be necessary to meet project deadlines. The hours of self-employed landscape architects vary depending on their workload.

Employment Figures

Landscape architects held about twenty-five thousand jobs in 2004. Two-thirds worked for firms that provide landscape architecture services. State and local governments were the next largest employers, and most of the rest were employed by architectural firms.

The federal government also employs landscape architects; most work for the U.S. Departments of Agriculture, Defense, and Interior. Approximately one of every four landscape architects is self-employed.

Most landscape architects work in urban and suburban areas in all parts of the country; some work in rural areas, particularly those in the federal government who plan and design parks and recreation areas.

Job Outlook

The concentration of new jobs tends to follow geographic improvements in the economy: Where business is booming, you'll find landscape architecture jobs. Possible employers include residential and commercial real estate developers, federal and state agencies, city planning departments, and individual property owners.

The U.S. Bureau of Labor Statistics reports that employment of landscape architects is expected to increase 27 percent or more through 2014. As the growing population continues to spur an increase in residential and commercial construction, landscape architects will be needed for the planning and development of many projects. With land costs rising and the public desiring more beautiful spaces, the importance of good site planning and landscape design is growing.

New construction is increasingly contingent on compliance with environmental regulations, zoning laws, and water restrictions. Landscape architects will be needed to help plan sites that meet these requirements and integrate new structures with the natural environment in the least disruptive way. The need to preserve and restore wetlands and other environmentally sensitive sites, as well as new demands to manage storm-water runoff in both existing and new landscapes, combined with the growing need to manage water resources in the Western states, should also lead to increased employment opportunities.

Continuation of the Transportation Equity Act for the Twenty-First Century (TEA-21) is also expected to spur employment for landscape architects, particularly through state and local governments. This act provides funds for the surface transportation and transit programs, such as interstate highway construction and maintenance, and environment-friendly pedestrian and bicycle trails.

In addition to the work related to new development and construction, landscape architects are expected to be involved in historic preservation (see Chapter 5), in land reclamation, and in refurbishment of existing sites. They are also doing more residential design work, as households spend more on landscaping than in the past.

Because landscape architects can work on many different types of projects, they may have an easier time finding employment than other design professionals when traditional construction slows down. During a recession, however, they may face layoffs and greater competition for jobs when property sales and construction slow down in some regions. Opportunities will vary from year to year and by geographic region, depending on the local economic conditions.

Although new graduates can expect to face competition for the plum jobs in the largest and most prestigious landscape architecture firms, they should nonetheless find good job opportunities overall as demand increases. Opportunities will be best for those who develop strong technical skills, such as computer design, and good communication skills. Familiarity with environmental codes and regulations is also important. Landscape architects with additional training or experience in urban planning increase their opportunities for employment in firms that specialize in site planning as well as landscape design. Many employers prefer to hire entry-level landscape architects who have internship experience because this significantly reduces the amount of on-the-job training required.

Traditionally, however, those who have landscape architecture training qualify for jobs as construction or landscape supervisors, landscape designers, drafters, land or environmental planners, or landscape consultants.

Salaries

Statistics are limited, but according to the U.S. Bureau of Labor Statistics, in 2004 the median annual earnings for landscape architects were $53,120. Most earned between $40,930 and $70,400, while the lowest 10 percent earned less than $32,390, and the highest 10 percent earned more than $90,850. Architectural, engineering, and related services employed more landscape architects than any other group of industries, and there the median annual earnings were $51,670.

In 2005 the average annual salary for all landscape architects in the federal government in nonsupervisory, supervisory, and managerial positions was $74,508.

A recent article in *Money* magazine ranked landscape architect as number thirty-four on a list of the fifty best jobs, citing an average annual salary of $50,500 and top earnings of $95,000.[1]

Because many landscape architects work for small firms or are self-employed, they receive less generous benefits than those with similar skills who work for large organizations. With the exception

1. Kalwarski, Tara, et al., "50 Best Jobs in America," *Money*, May 2006, p. 94.

of those who are self-employed, however, most landscape architects receive health insurance, paid vacations, and sick leave.

A Landscape Architect at Work

Matthew I. Zehnder, senior vice president of landscape architecture and community planning, works for META Associates, Inc., in Louisville, Kentucky, a health care–oriented strategic planning and program management firm that is part of the Parsons Commercial Technology Group. The firm deals primarily with all developmental aspects of health care–related projects, from the master planning of health care–assisted living communities to forty-bed private-care facilities.

Zehnder was attracted to landscape architecture because he enjoyed working with plants and was interested in learning how to implement a design using plants as a palette. He also liked the possibility of occasionally working outdoors. He earned his bachelor of science degree in landscape architecture from the University of Kentucky in Lexington and a master's degree in landscape architecture and regional planning from the University of Pennsylvania in Philadelphia.

Getting Started

Zehnder researched several firms in the community where he wanted to live, learning as much as possible about each one. He also learned about the firms' partners so that he would be well informed if invited for an interview.

A midlevel executive from META Associates asked if he would be interested in leading the company's planning department. Zehnder was very interested in the offer and began what turned out to be a six-month interview process. He used the separate interviews with each of the firm's three partners to express his views and ideas concerning design and to market himself.

In the next step of the interview process, the partners asked Zehnder to draft a business plan and forecast a billable figure for his first year with the firm. This was followed by a final interview, during which he presented his requirements for employment. Negotiations following this meeting culminated in a written offer that Zehnder accepted.

Job Description

Zehnder enthusiastically states that he loves his job. He is able to set his own hours, answers to one partner, and is responsible for his own work. The job is a bit unusual because it includes marketing and contractual administration, which isn't the path generally followed by most landscape architects.

A typical day begins at 9:00 A.M., when Zehnder answers messages and writes notes to business associates and friends who are part of his professional network. He believes strongly in the value of maintaining a network of colleagues and friends who can have a positive influence on his career. As he says, "The three most important words in business are network, network, network!"

Zehnder doesn't spend much time drawing, having chosen executive management over drafting. He explains that many landscape architects continue to do drafting for a living throughout their careers. This doesn't mean that they haven't advanced in the field; landscape architecture is a profession in which you can set your own goals and work in whichever area you choose.

If he's not working on a proposal for a project, Zehnder is completing a schematic design or making appointments to visit potential clients. On average, he works about sixty-five hours a week and doesn't bring any work home. The job also includes frequent travel to job sites. Since the firm competes on a national level, he estimates that he logs around 120,000 flight miles a year.

Zehnder enjoys the friendly atmosphere of the office, as well as the constructive criticism that colleagues offer to one another on their designs. The job allows him a good deal of freedom, and he appreciates the trust his employer has in him and his work. He finds paperwork to be the least enjoyable part of the job.

Zehnder's philosophy about his career is a simple one: he says that he will continue to work and do a good job for his employer as long as he enjoys what he does. When he no longer enjoys the job, he will look for new opportunities.

Professional Advice

Zehnder offers some helpful advice to aspiring landscape architects. "Know what you want to do in life—where you want to be," he says. "It is essential to write down a set of goals to reach in five years and continue to review your goals and adjust them as necessary.

"You must network with all types of people, and you must decide between the academic world and the professional world of this profession. They are two very different worlds.

"Pick the firm you want to work for and pursue it like it's the last place in the world to work. And the most important thing—believe in what you want to do and do it!"

2

TRAINING FOR LANDSCAPE ARCHITECTS

LANDSCAPE ARCHITECTS ARE highly trained professionals. If you're considering a career in this field, you'll need to know precisely what kind of education and training will make you most attractive to potential employers. In this chapter we'll explore the educational and licensing requirements you'll need, as well as the personal attributes that will add to your professional success.

Degrees Needed

A bachelor's or master's degree in landscape architecture is generally the minimum educational requirement for entry positions. A bachelor's of landscape architecture (B.L.A.) degree takes four or five years to complete; a master's degree takes two or three years.

There are two types of accredited master's degree programs. The more common is a three-year first professional degree program designed for students with an undergraduate degree in another discipline. The second type of master's degree is a two-year second professional degree program, intended for students who have a bachelor's degree in landscape architecture and who wish to teach or specialize in some aspect of the field, such as regional planning or golf course design.

Choosing a Program

In 2004 fifty-nine colleges and universities in the United States and Canada offered eighty-four undergraduate and graduate programs in landscape architecture that were accredited by the Landscape Architecture Accreditation Board of the American Society of Landscape Architects (ASLA).

When choosing your program, be sure to find out whether the school you're considering is accredited and what its specialization is. Contact the ASLA for information on accredited programs (see Appendix A).

Course of Study

Your college curriculum will include the following courses.

- Civil engineering, including grading and drainage and pipe design
- Construction law and contracts
- Design and color theory
- Drafting

- General management
- Geology
- History of landscape architecture
- Landscape design and construction
- Landscape ecology
- Meteorology
- Plant and soil science and introductory horticulture courses
- Soil science
- Structural design
- Surveying
- Topography
- Urban and regional planning

In addition, most students at the undergraduate level take a year of prerequisite courses such as English, mathematics, and social and physical sciences.

The design studio is an important aspect of many landscape architecture programs. Whenever possible, students are assigned real projects to work on, providing them with valuable hands-on experience. Working on these projects may help you to become more proficient in the use of technologies such as computer-aided design, geographic information systems, and video simulation.

Going on for a master's degree will help you refine your design abilities and focus on more complex types of design problems. It will also add greatly to your employability and salary prospects.

Sample Program

Following is a summary of the landscape architecture program offered at California Polytechnic in San Luis Obispo. It's offered as an example of what you can expect to find in an undergraduate degree program.

The department of landscape architecture is part of the College of Architecture and Environmental Design. The bachelor of landscape architecture is a five-year degree program with a strong environmental analysis and design core based on a foundation of courses in the arts, sciences, and humanities. Through frequent involvement in real projects, students have opportunities to experience sites and clients with relevant contemporary issues and problems. Areas of study and investigation include the following.

- Applied sciences
- Graphics and visual communication
- Human values and environmental sensitivity
- Landscape analysis, assessment, and planning
- Landscape construction
- Landscape ecology
- Landscape history and theory
- Professional practice
- Site planning and design
- Technology—use and integration
- Urban and community design

Students develop professional teamwork and interdisciplinary practice skills through team teaching, student teamwork, and collaboration with other disciplines within the College of Architecture and Environmental Design and the university. They develop a global perspective of the profession through opportunities for international study and travel as well as the ongoing integration of multicultural and diverse environmental issues in course work.

Licensing

At this time, forty-six states and two Canadian provinces require landscape architects to be licensed or registered. Check with your state or province for the current status of its requirements.

Licensing for both U.S. and Canadian landscape architects is based on the Landscape Architect Registration Examination (LARE), sponsored by the Council of Landscape Architectural Registration Boards. The exam consists of two portions, graphic and multiple choice; each part of the test is administered over two days. Although state requirements may differ, admission to the exam usually requires a degree from an accredited school plus one to four years of work experience under the supervision of a registered landscape architect. Currently fourteen states require that a candidate for licensure pass a state examination in addition to the LARE. State exams focus on laws, environmental regulations, plants, soils, climate, and any other characteristics unique to the state. These exams are usually one hour in length and are completed at the end of the LARE.

Because state requirements for licensure aren't uniform, you may find it difficult to transfer your registration from one state to another. However, if you meet the national standards of graduating from an accredited program, serving three years of internship under the supervision of a registered landscape architect, and passing the LARE, you can satisfy requirements in most states and can obtain certification from the Council of Landscape Architectural Registration Boards and so gain reciprocity (the right to work) in other states.

In states where licensure is required, you'll be called an apprentice or intern landscape architect until you become licensed. Your duties will vary depending on the type and size of the firm you work for. You may do research for projects or prepare working drawings, construction documents, or base maps of the area to be landscaped. Some firms may allow you to participate in the actual design of a project. Whatever your assigned duties, however, as an intern you must perform all work under the supervision of a licensed landscape architect. Additionally, all drawings and specifications must be signed and sealed by the licensed professional, who takes legal responsibility for the work.

Licensure for landscape architects employed by the federal government is not required; however, candidates who aspire to entry positions should have a bachelor's or master's degree in landscape architecture.

Personal Qualities

If you're planning to pursue a career in landscape architecture, you should appreciate nature, enjoy working with your hands, and possess strong analytical skills. Creative vision and artistic talent are desirable, but they aren't essential for success. However, good oral communication skills are vital because you'll have to convey your ideas to other professionals and clients and make presentations before large groups. You'll also need strong writing skills.

Knowledge of all kinds of computer applications, including word processing, desktop publishing, and spreadsheets, is a vital skill. Landscape architects use these tools to develop presentations, proposals, reports, and land impact studies for clients, colleagues, and superiors. The ability to draft and design using CAD software is essential.

Many employers recommend that you complete at least one summer internship with a landscape architecture firm to gain an understanding of the day-to-day operations of a small business, including how to win clients, generate fees, and work within a budget. If you think you'd like to start your own company, courses in small business management will be a great help.

Related Job Titles

There are many disciplines with a wide variety of job titles that are related to the field of landscape architecture. They range from those open to the unskilled laborer with little or no experience and training to the master's-degree-level professional, as well as all the steps in between. The remainder of part one of this book will examine the following job titles:

- Urban and regional planner
- Forester
- Conservationist
- Historic landscape preservationist
- Garden historian
- Landscape archaeologist
- Topiary trainer
- Landscape designer
- Gardener
- Groundskeeper
- Arborist
- Golf course manager
- Cemetery worker

3

URBAN AND REGIONAL PLANNING

URBAN AND REGIONAL planners develop long- and short-term land-use plans to provide for growth and revitalization of urban, suburban, and rural communities, while helping local officials make decisions on social, economic, and environmental problems. They are often referred to as community or city planners because many are employed by local governments.

These professionals devise plans promoting the best use of a community's land and resources for residential, commercial, and recreational activities. They're also involved in various other planning activities, including social services, transportation, resource development, and the protection of ecologically sensitive regions.

Urban planners address issues such as traffic congestion, air pollution, and the effect of growth and change on an area. They may formulate capital improvement plans for the construction of new school buildings, public housing, or sewage systems.

Planners are involved in environmental issues ranging from pollution control to wetland preservation, forest conservation, and the location of new landfills. They may also be involved with drafting legislation on social issues such as the needs of the elderly, sheltering the homeless, meeting the demand for new correctional facilities, and so forth.

Duties of Planners

Urban and regional planners examine proposed community facilities, such as schools, to be sure that they will meet the demands placed on them over time by population growth. They keep abreast of the economic and legal issues concerning zoning codes, building codes, and environmental regulations and ensure that builders and developers follow these rules.

Planners also deal with land-use and environmental issues created by population movements. For example, as suburban growth increases the need for commuting, some planners design new transportation systems and parking facilities.

Before preparing plans for community development, planners report on the current use of land for residential, business, and community purposes. These reports include information on the location of streets, highways, water and sewer lines, schools, libraries, and cultural and recreational sites; they also provide data on the types of industries in the community, characteristics of the population, and employment and economic trends. With this information, along with input from citizens' advisory committees, planners design the layout of recommended buildings and other facilities, such as subway lines and stations, for example, and prepare reports that show how their programs can be carried out and what they will cost.

Getting the Job Done

Planners use computers to record and analyze information and to prepare their reports and recommendations for government leaders and others. Computer databases, spreadsheets, and analytical techniques are widely used to determine program costs and forecast future trends in employment, housing, transportation, or population. Computerized geographic information systems enable planners to map land areas and overlay maps with geographic variables, such as population density, as well as to combine and manipulate geographic information to produce alternative plans for land use or development.

Urban and regional planners often confer with land developers, civic leaders, and public officials. They may function as mediators in community disputes by presenting alternatives that are acceptable to opposing parties. Planners may prepare material for community relations programs, speak at civic meetings, and appear before legislative committees and elected officials to explain and defend their proposals.

Those employed by large organizations usually specialize in a single area such as transportation, housing, historic preservation, urban design, environmental and regulatory issues, or economic development. Planners working in small organizations must be generalists who are able to do various tasks.

Working Conditions

Urban and regional planners spend much of their time in offices, but they periodically work outdoors, inspecting the features of land under consideration for development, including its current use and the types of structures on it.

Some local government planners involved in site development inspections spend most of their time in the field. Although most planners work a forty-hour workweek, they frequently attend evening or weekend meetings or public hearings with citizens' groups.

Planners may experience the pressure of deadlines and tight work schedules, as well as political pressure generated by special interest groups affected by their land-use proposals.

Job Settings

Urban and regional planners hold about thirty-two thousand jobs; two out of three are employed by local governments. An increasing number are employed in the private sector, finding work with architectural and engineering firms as well as with companies that provide management, scientific, and technical consulting services. Others work for state government agencies dealing with housing, transportation, or environmental protection. A small number of planners are employed by the federal government.

Many planners do consulting work, providing services to private developers or government agencies either part-time as a supplement to their regular jobs or as full-time employment. Private sector employers include architectural and surveying firms, management and public relations firms, educational institutions, large land developers, and law firms specializing in land use.

Training

You'll need a master's degree for most entry-level jobs in urban and regional planning to have the advanced training preferred by most employers. To qualify for an entry-level job at any level of government, a master's degree from an accredited program in urban or regional planning or a master's degree in a related field, such as urban design or geography, is required.

A master's degree from an accredited planning program will provide you with the best training for a wide range of planning fields. A limited number of schools offer accredited bachelor's degree programs in planning, but you'll still need a graduate degree to advance beyond entry-level positions. You should also take classes in related disciplines, such as architecture, law, earth sciences, demography, economics, finance, health administration, geographic information systems, and management. Courses in statistics and computer science are also recommended because familiarity with computer models and statistical techniques is important in planning.

About sixty-eight colleges and universities offer an accredited master's degree program in urban or regional planning, and fifteen offer an accredited bachelor's degree program. Accreditation is granted by the Planning Accreditation Board, which consists of representatives of the American Institute of Certified Planners, the American Planning Association, and the Association of Collegiate Schools of Planning. Most graduate programs in planning require a minimum of two years of study. In Canada, the Canadian Institute of Planners accredits nineteen master's degree programs and nine bachelor's degree programs.

Your specialized courses of study in most planning programs are environmental planning, land-use and comprehensive planning, economic development, housing, historic preservation, and social planning. Other popular offerings include community development, transportation, and urban design. As a graduate student, you'll spend considerable time in studios, workshops, and laboratory courses learning to analyze and solve planning problems.

Depending on the particular program, you may be required to work in a planning office part-time or during the summer. Local government planning offices frequently offer student internships, providing you experience that proves invaluable in securing a full-time planning position after graduation.

The American Institute of Certified Planners, a professional institute within the American Planning Association, grants certification to individuals who have the appropriate combination of education and professional experience and who pass an examination. The Canadian Institute of Planners also grants certification to those who meet its requirements. Certification may be helpful when seeking promotion.

Personal Qualities

To be a successful urban planner, you should be able to think in terms of spatial relationships and visualize the effects of your plans and designs. You'll need to be flexible, able to reconcile different viewpoints, and able to make constructive policy recommendations. Your ability to write and speak clearly will also be an important part of your work.

Opportunities for Advancement

After a few years' experience, planners may advance to assignments requiring a high degree of independent judgment, such as designing the physical layout of a large development or recommending policy and budget options. Some public sector planners are promoted to jobs as planning directors and spend a great deal of time meeting with officials, speaking to civic groups, and supervising a staff. Further advancement is possible through a transfer to a larger jurisdiction with more complex problems and greater responsibilities or into related occupations, such as director of community or economic development. In the private sector, experience leads to increases in independence and compensation.

Salaries

Salaries of planners vary by level of education, type of employer, experience, size of community in which they work, and geographic location. Median annual earnings of urban and regional planners were $53,450 in 2004, with most earning between $41,950 and $67,530. The lowest 10 percent earned less than $33,840, and the highest 10 percent earned more than $82,610. Local government employed the largest number of planners, whose median annual earnings were $52,520.

In 2006 the federal government hired applicants with bachelor's degrees in urban planning at a starting salary of $45,062; those with master's degrees were offered a starting salary of $65,048.

Job Outlook for Urban and Regional Planners

A master's degree from an accredited program should give you an advantage in the job market over those with a bachelor's degree. Overall, employment of urban and regional planners is expected to increase up to 17 percent through at least 2014. This projected increase will be driven by the need for state and local governments to provide public services, such as regulation of commercial development, the environment, transportation, and housing, and land-use and development for an expanding population.

While initiatives from the private sector dealing with historic preservation and redevelopment will provide additional openings, most new jobs for urban and regional planners will be in local government, as planners will be needed to address an array of problems associated with population growth, especially in affluent, rapidly expanding communities. For example, new housing developments require roads, sewer systems, fire stations, schools, libraries, and recreation facilities that must be planned for within the consideration of budgetary constraints. Small-town chambers of commerce, economic development authorities, and tourism bureaus may also hire planners, preferably those with some background in marketing and public relations.

The fastest job growth for urban and regional planners should occur in the private sector, primarily in professional, scientific, and technical services. As an example, these firms may employ planners to help design security measures for a building that meet a desired security level but that are also subtle and blend in with the surrounding area. However, because the private sector employs fewer than two out of ten urban and regional planners, not as many new jobs will be created in the private sector as in government.

An Urban and Regional Planner at Work

Cliff Davidson is an urban and regional transportation planner with the Grand Junction/Mesa County Metropolitan Planning Organization (MPO), Mesa County Government in Grand Junction, Colorado. He earned his bachelor of science degree in city and regional planning from California Polytechnic University in San Luis Obispo. He has also been trained in transportation modeling, geographic information systems (GIS), cartography, surveying, and graphic design.

Davidson's attraction to urban planning actually began in child-hood, when he spent time building model cities and railroads. He loved creating environments for cars, highways, buildings, bridges, and the people he imagined would use them. His career decision was made by age nine.

Davidson likes to see communities work better. He wanted to help democracy at the local government level and do his part to change the world for the better by the way a town develops and expands over time. He found it easy to teach the basics of planning to others, particularly locally appointed planning commissioners, and to explain why planning saves money, how it creates safer and more livable neighborhoods, and how it can make communities more attractive to good industries for jobs.

Getting Started

After graduating from Cal Poly, Davidson decided to travel. He headed east, stopping in Texas while the Dallas–Ft. Worth Regional Airport was being built. Davidson decided to stay in Dallas and began auditing classes in the Urban Affairs Program at the University of Texas at Arlington. The county needed a planner to help all the small communities in the area cope with the new development spurred by the airport construction, and Davidson's instructors submitted his name to the county as an applicant for the position. Since there weren't many degreed planners in the area at that time, the county hired Davidson right away. His initial responsibilities included small-town planning, park designs, and running training courses for several smaller communities.

Davidson considers his combined training in planning and GIS to be a good foundation for his career, since planning requires layers of land information to make sound decisions. Planners study soils, topography, floodplains, zoning, proximity to schools and shopping, and access to public services and facilities such as roads, water, and sewers.

All of this used to be done by manually mapping each layer of information on a sheet of acetate and overlaying one on top of the next to establish patterns. However, with GIS technology this is done automatically, and each layer is displayed on the computer screen and plotter to produce analytical maps. A geographic information system is a computerized mapping system that stores both the map and the data together in one computer file. This means that a road is both a line on the map as well as a data table that tells the user how wide the road is, whether it's paved, its name and classification, the number of lanes, the amount of traffic it carries, and so forth.

Davidson became interested in GIS after working for Mesa County for about five years. He was working in the county's computer department, installing microcomputers and training county personnel on new technology. He was then transferred into the Public Works Department to create the first electronic base map and census file for the county. After working as a cartographic analyst for two years and creating the new Mesa County GIS, he was promoted to administrator, making him the head of the Metropolitan Planning Organization.

Davidson explains that GIS is not a profession but a tool that can be used by people working in many fields. Soil scientists, geologists, sociologists, businesspeople, postmasters, road supervisors, census takers, demographers, engineers, and transportation planners use it. Much of his time is spent teaching staff members and other agencies how to best use GIS for their particular activities, such as housing, utilities, surveying, or fire and police protection.

Davidson has actually had many jobs in his career with Mesa County. From his initial duties as land-use planner, he has worked as graphic artist, microcomputer manager, cartographic analyst, and administrator. In each position he continued to study technology to come up with solutions to a range of county problems.

Job Description

Davidson says that a planner's job entails hours of research on development projects and the issues surrounding them, including the ability to provide services to the development and the land's ability to accommodate the proposed project. It can take many months to complete the research needed to develop a comprehensive plan, which is a document and set of maps showing what the community could or should look like in twenty years based on present trends, population growth, water availability, geologic constraints, and the transportation system's capacity. Since the planner has to produce many sets of maps and reports, strong writing and graphics skills are essential.

While developing a comprehensive plan, the planner meets with developers, landowners, citizens, and elected representatives. The planner's findings are presented in private meetings and open public hearings. Since large development projects are often emotional issues within a community, Davidson warns that the planner is "always the bad guy" to one side or the other. Sometimes elected officials appreciate the planner's work and support the project; other times they are against it and often voice their displeasure openly in public meetings. Davidson advises making technical, professional presentations devoid of personal opinions, letting the maps, graphics, and written documents state the case without bias.

Davidson spends between thirty and eighty hours a week on the job, depending on what deadlines he is facing on projects. He tries to schedule his work to avoid all-night sessions, but deadlines are sometimes changed or problems arise when policy changes or a natural disaster occurs. "One thing I have never been in twenty-four years in this kind of job is bored," he says.

One of the things Davidson enjoys most about his work is meeting new people and having an impact on the community. He also likes the technical side, producing maps and reports. He enjoys the challenge of making maps that show the different elements he's trying to communicate, such as traffic volumes, school bus routes, or the location of sidewalks and bicycle paths.

On the downside, Davidson doesn't like the unavoidable conflicts he must face with petitioners for developers and elected or appointed officials. He also dislikes seeing hard work go to waste when politics takes precedence over rational thought. This doesn't happen very often, though, especially if the planner has been thorough in preparing research, analysis, and the presentation of the proposal.

Professional Advice

Davidson has some specific advice for anyone interested in a career in community planning. He strongly recommends getting an undergraduate degree in planning as well as serving an internship to learn right off what the work is really like. While a master's degree in planning may get you a slightly higher salary in your first job, Davidson believes that the experience you'll receive in a good planning program is a solid foundation for your first position.

Davidson stresses that you need to love creating maps and graphics that communicate your plan. He suggests some additional skills that will help you excel in this area, including demographics, cartography, computer graphics, spreadsheet analysis, database development, and research techniques.

Since reports and presentations are vital to a planner's work, you should love to write and be comfortable speaking before an audience. The ability to use logic and persuasion is also important.

Finally, Davidson recommends becoming involved in the PTA, civic groups, or a community design project—any experience working with people to get from inception to a built product. "You have to basically like being around many different kinds of people—you have to find something to like in all of them—in order to enjoy this kind of work," he says.

4

FORESTRY AND CONSERVATION

FORESTS AND RANGELANDS serve a variety of needs. They supply wood products, livestock forage, minerals, and water; serve as sites for recreational activities; and provide habitats for wildlife. Foresters and conservation scientists manage, develop, use, and help protect these and other natural resources.

Foresters, Range Managers, and Soil Conservationists

Although many professional foresters and forest technicians spend most of their time working outdoors during the first few years of their career, there are some who do not.

Duties outdoors include:

- Measuring and grading trees
- Evaluating insect outbreaks
- Conducting land surveys
- Fighting wildfires
- Laying out road systems
- Supervising construction of trails
- Planting trees
- Supervising timber harvesting
- Conducting research studies

After a few years of on-the-ground experience, foresters can advance to administrative positions and then spend less time outside. Administrative duties include:

- Planning
- Contracting
- Preparing reports
- Managing budgets
- Consulting

A professional forester has earned a four-year degree, while a forest technician normally holds an associate's degree in forest technology. Foresters concentrate on management skills, policy decisions, and the application of ecological concepts. Technicians generally accomplish day-to-day tasks working under the supervision of a professional forester.

Range managers, also called range conservationists, range ecologists, or range scientists, manage, improve, and protect rangelands to maximize their use without damaging the environment.

Soil conservationists provide technical assistance to farmers and others concerned with the conservation of soil, water, and related natural resources. They develop programs to get the most use out of the land without damaging it.

Training

Seventeen states have mandatory licensing and/or voluntary registration requirements that you must meet to acquire the title "professional forester" and practice forestry in the state. Both licensing and registration requirements usually entail completing a four-year degree in forestry and several years of forestry work experience. Candidates pursuing licensing also may be required to pass a comprehensive written exam.

In Canada, nine universities offer qualified degrees, and community colleges throughout the country offer various forestry programs at the diploma level. Check with your provincial institute of forestry for specific requirements. The Canadian Institute of Forestry promotes competence among forestry professionals by offering continuing education and maintaining a code of ethics.

Most land-grant colleges and universities offer a bachelor's and/or a master's degree in forestry. The Society of American Foresters accredits approximately forty-eight such programs throughout the United States. Your curriculum will stress four components: forest ecology and biology, measurement of forest resources, management of forest resources, and public policy. You should plan to balance general science courses such as ecology, biology, tree physiology, taxonomy, and soil formation with technical forestry courses such as forest inventory or wildlife habitat assessment, remote sensing, land surveying, global positioning systems (GPS) technology, integrated forest resource management, silviculture, and forest protection. Mathematics, statistics, and computer science courses also are recommended.

Many forestry programs include advanced computer applications such as global information systems (GIS) and resource assessment programs. Classes in resource policy and administration, specifically forest economics and business administration, will supplement your scientific and technical knowledge. In most programs, you will also study best management practices, wetlands analysis, and sustainability and regulatory issues, in response to the growing focus on protecting forested lands during timber harvesting operations.

To work as a forester, you should have a strong grasp of federal, state, and local policy issues and of the increasingly numerous and complex environmental regulations that affect many forestry-related activities. Many colleges will require you to complete a field session either in a camp operated by the college or in a cooperative work-study program with a federal or state agency or with private industry. All schools will encourage you to take summer jobs that provide experience in forestry or conservation work.

Conservation scientists generally hold a minimum of a bachelor's degree in fields such as ecology, natural resource management, agriculture, biology, environmental science, or another related field. A master's or Ph.D. degree is usually required for teaching and research positions.

Most range managers have a degree in range management or range science. Nine schools offer degrees that are accredited by the Society of Range Management, and more than forty others offer course work in range science or in a closely related discipline with a range management or range science option. Your specialized range management courses will combine plant, animal, and soil sciences with principles of ecology and resource management. In addition, you should take electives including economics, statistics, forestry, hydrology, agronomy, wildlife, animal husbandry, computer science, and recreation. Selection of a minor in range management, such as wildlife ecology, watershed management, animal science, or agricultural economics, can often enhance your qualifications for certain types of employment.

The Society for Range Management offers two types of certification: one as a certified professional in rangeland management (CPRM) and another as a certified range management consultant. To be considered a candidate for certification, you must have at least a bachelor's degree in range science or a closely related field combined with a minimum of six years of full-time work experience, and you must pass a comprehensive written exam.

The Society of American Foresters has a certified forester program. To become certified, you'll need to have at least a bachelor's degree from a forestry program accredited by the society or one that is substantially equivalent. You also must have five years of qualifying professional experience and pass an examination.

Additionally, if you've taken the proper course work in college, you can seek certification as a wetland scientist through the Society of Wetland Scientists and certification as a professional wildlife biologist through the Wildlife Society.

Very few colleges and universities offer degrees in soil conservation. Most soil conservationists have degrees in environmental studies, agronomy, general agriculture, hydrology, or crop or soil science; a few have degrees in related fields such as wildlife biology, forestry, and range management. Programs of study usually include thirty semester hours in natural resources or agriculture, including at least three hours in soil science.

In addition to meeting the demands of forestry and conservation research and analysis, you should enjoy working outdoors, be able to tolerate extensive walking and other types of physical exertion, and be willing to move to where the jobs are. You should also be able to work well with people and have good communication skills.

Recent forestry and conservation science graduates usually work under the supervision of experienced foresters or scientists. After gaining experience, they may advance to more responsible positions. In the federal government, most entry-level positions are in forest resource management. An experienced federal forester may supervise a ranger district and may advance to forest supervisor, regional forester, or perhaps to a top administrative position in the national headquarters.

As a forester working in private industry, you'll start by learning the practical and administrative aspects of the business and acquiring comprehensive technical training and then be introduced to contract writing, timber harvesting, and decision making. You may work your way up to top managerial positions and once in management will probably leave the fieldwork behind, spending more time in an office working with teams to develop management plans and supervising others. After gaining several years of experience, you may become a consulting forester, working alone or with one or several partners. Consulting foresters contract with state or local governments, private landowners, private industry, or other forestry consulting groups.

Soil conservationists usually begin working within one county or conservation district and, with experience, may advance to the area, state, regional, or national level. They can also transfer to related occupations, such as farm or ranch management advisor or land appraiser.

Finding a Job

You can find information about various aspects of careers in forestry, range management, and soil conservation from a number of sources, some of which are listed in Appendix A. In addition, *Conservation Directory* is an annual publication by the National Wildlife Federation that lists, by states and Canadian provinces, the organizations, agencies, and officials concerned with natural resource use and management. It's available free online, or a print version can be purchased from the National Wildlife Federation. Visit www.nwf.org/conservationdirectory for information.

The *Journal of Forestry* is a monthly publication listing employment opportunities. It's free to Society of American Forester members. On the Web, go to www.safnet.org/periodicals/journal.cfm for more information.

The Environmental Career Center is an online resource that lists hundreds of jobs in environmental fields. The service is free to registered users and is located at www.environmentalcareer.com.

Job Outlook

Employment of conservation scientists and foresters is expected to increase only as much as 8 percent for all occupations through at least 2014, with the highest growth expected in private sector consulting firms. Demand should be spurred by a continuing emphasis on environmental protection, responsible land management, and water-related issues. Growing interest in developing private lands and forests for recreational purposes will generate additional jobs for foresters and conservation scientists. Fire prevention is another area of growth for these two occupations.

Conservation scientists should find employment as a result of increasing government regulations, such as those regarding the management of storm water and coastlines, which have created demand for professionals to manage runoff and erosion on farms and in cities and suburbs. Soil and water quality experts will be needed as states design initiatives to improve water resources by preventing pollution by agricultural producers and industrial plants.

Overall employment in this field is expected to decline slightly in the federal government, mostly because of budgetary constraints and the trend among all levels of government toward contracting these functions to private consulting firms. Also, federal land management agencies, such as the USDA Forest Service, have deemphasized their timber programs and increasingly focused on wildlife, recreation, and sustaining ecosystems, thereby spurring demand for other life and social scientists rather than for foresters. Despite this fact, many jobs should be created by the number of foresters who retire or leave government employment for other reasons. At the state level, governments are expected to increase their hiring of conservation scientists and foresters as their budgetary situations improve. A small number of new jobs are expected to result from the need for range and soil conservationists to provide technical assistance to owners of grazing land through the Natural Resource Conservation Service.

Foresters involved with timber harvesting should find good opportunities in the Southeast, where much forested land is privately owned. However, the recent opening of public lands to commercial activity, especially in the West, will also help the outlook for foresters. Salaried foresters working for private industry, such as paper companies, sawmills, and pulpwood mills, will be needed to provide technical assistance and management plans to landowners. Consulting foresters should also find work in this area.

The demand for professionals to prepare environmental impact statements and erosion and sediment control plans, to monitor water quality near logging sites, and to advise on tree harvesting practices required by government regulations have led scientific research and development services to increase their hiring of foresters and conservation scientists in recent years. This trend is expected to continue over the next several years.

Salaries

In 2005 most bachelor's degree graduates entering the federal government as foresters, range managers, or soil conservationists started between $24,677 and $30,567 annually, depending on their academic achievement. Those with a master's degree started between $37,390 and $45,239. Holders of doctorates started at $54,221. Beginning salaries were slightly higher in selected areas where the prevailing local pay level was higher. In 2005 the average federal salary for foresters in nonsupervisory, supervisory, and managerial positions was $63,492; for soil conservationists, $60,671; and for rangeland managers, $58,162.

According to the National Association of Colleges and Employers, graduates with a bachelor's degree in conservation and renewable natural resources received an average starting salary offer of $27,950 in 2005.

In private industry, starting salaries for graduates with a bachelor's degree were comparable with starting salaries in the federal government, but starting salaries in state and local governments were usually lower. Conservation scientists and foresters who work for federal, state, and local governments and large private firms generally receive more generous benefits than do those working for smaller firms.

Conservation scientists overall had median annual earnings of $52,480 in 2004; most earned between $39,660 and $65,550. The lowest 10 percent earned less than $30,740, and the highest 10 percent earned more than $78,470.

Median annual earnings of foresters were $48,230 in 2004; the majority earned between $37,260 and $60,500. Those in the lowest 10 percent earned less than $29,770, and the highest 10 percent earned more than $72,050.

National Park Service Rangers

The National Park Service, a bureau of the U.S. Department of the Interior, maintains more than 370 sites across the United States and in Guam, Puerto Rico, and the Virgin Islands. These encompass natural and recreational areas, including the Grand Canyon and Yellowstone National Parks; sites that preserve the nation's cultural and historical treasures, such as Gettysburg Battlefield; and parks that represent national beauty along waterlines, such as Lake Mead.

Most sites aren't located near major cities, so serious candidates must, for the most part, be prepared to relocate. In addition, most rangers are assigned to several different parts of the country throughout their careers. Housing may or may not be provided, depending on the site and your position.

The National Park Service hires three categories of park rangers (generally on a seasonal basis): enforcement, general, and interpretation. Most jobs in forestry, range management, and soil conservation are in the general category.

Duties vary greatly from position to position and from site to site, but rangers in the general division are usually responsible for forestry or resource management; developing and presenting programs that explain a park's historic, cultural, or archaeological features; campground maintenance; firefighting; lifeguarding; law enforcement; and search and rescue.

Rangers also sit at information desks, provide visitor services, or participate in conservation or restoration projects. Entry-level employees might also collect fees, provide first aid, and operate audiovisual equipment.

Qualifications and Salaries

The National Park Service weighs several factors in determining a candidate's eligibility for employment and at which salary level he or she will start. In essence, those with the least experience or education will begin at the lowest federal government salary grade of GS-2. Based on the 2006 GS rates, the current salary for this grade is $18,385, but the requirements are only six months of experience in related work or a high school diploma or its equivalent.

The more related work experience or education an applicant brings, the higher the salary level. For example, GS-4 requires either eighteen months of general experience in park operations or in related fields and six months of specialized experience, or one ninety-day season as a seasonal park ranger at the GS-3 level. The current GS-4 salary is $22,519.

Getting Your Foot in the Door

Competition is stiff for park ranger positions, so only the most qualified applicants will be selected. You will have a better chance for success if you have an undergraduate degree in natural resource management, natural or earth sciences, history, archaeology, anthropology, park and recreation management, law enforcement or police science, social or behavioral sciences, museum sciences, business or public administration, or sociology. Studying other closely related subjects that pertain to the management and protection of natural and cultural resources and related applicable job experiences are also considered beneficial.

The best way for a newcomer to break in is to start off with seasonal employment during school breaks. With a couple of summer seasons under your belt, the doors will open more easily for permanent employment.

Because of Office of Personnel Management regulations, veterans of the U.S. Armed Forces have a decided advantage. Depending on their experience, they may be given preference.

How to Apply

Recruitment for temporary seasonal employment is open year-round, and you may apply for positions at any park maintained by the National Park Service. Applications for seasonal employment may also be completed online at www.nps.gov.

Parks Canada Wardens

Parks Canada is the agency that maintains the national parks, historic sites, and marine conservation areas of Canada. Parks Canada protects and preserves the natural and cultural resources found in the country's parks. The agency employs people nationwide in permanent, full-time, part-time, temporary, and seasonal jobs. Many opportunities also exist for student employment.

The Warden Service is the branch of Parks Canada that employs about 450 park wardens, the Canadian equivalent of park rangers. A warden's responsibilities include protecting and maintaining natural resources, preventing or responding to forest fires and floods, enforcing the National Parks Act, and communicating with the public.

Qualifications

A university degree in natural resources is the minimum education requirement for a career as a park warden. In addition, you must be physically fit and able to travel and work in different environments.

Experience in wilderness travel using a variety of personal and technical equipment is helpful. This might include familiarity with global positioning systems or knowledge of rock climbing. Experience in natural resource management, public safety, or law enforcement is also beneficial. You'll need good communication skills, since a park warden interacts regularly with a variety of people. You must also have a valid driver's license as well as first-aid and CPR certificates, and you'll be required to pass a preemployment medical exam and security check.

Competition for park warden positions is strong, and there is limited outside recruitment for entry-level positions. Parks Canada normally conducts entry-level competitions once a year, in late summer and early fall, at various locations throughout the country. These positions are for seasonal and term employment; advancement to a permanent position is achieved through service.

In general when a park warden competition is posted, the applications that meet the required qualifications are forwarded to Parks Canada. In addition to a written exam and interview, successful candidates must complete the eleven-week Recruit Warden Training Program. Upon completion of this in-residence program, the candidate will be offered a position in a park, where completion of the field training portion of the program is required.

Related Professions

Foresters and conservation scientists are not the only workers who manage, develop, and protect natural resources. Other workers with similar responsibilities include agricultural scientists, agricultural engineers, biological scientists, environmental scientists, farm and ranch managers, soil scientists and soil conservation technicians, and wildlife managers.

A Forester at Work

Mark T. Folwell is a forester working as a wood-yard foreman with Temple Inland Forest Company in Lula, Georgia.

Folwell became interested in forestry after working at numerous jobs that he realized didn't offer him any future security. He began hiking and camping with a friend, and loved his time in the outdoors so much that he decided to pursue forestry as a profession. Although he initially thought forestry would be an easy job consisting of some walks through the woods and an occasional deer sighting, he was faced with reality very quickly. While he's certainly seen deer, he's also had to deal with yellow jackets, snakes, and all kinds of insects. Walks through the woods are often done in extreme heat, and Folwell has to be careful not to step into a stump hole or a well. Since he must meet a quota on how much acreage he covers, he has to move quickly but very carefully.

Folwell's job has taught him a deep respect for the woods and for nature, showing him a beauty that he believes can't be seen from a car window on a country drive. He feels a great sense of accomplishment at the end of a day when he has safely completed his assignments; although he's tired and has aching muscles, he's content knowing that his work is for the benefit of everyone involved with wood products.

Getting Started

Folwell studied at Lake City Forest Ranger School in Lake City, Florida. He chose the school because it offered a two-year program and he had little money and time to spend, wanting to complete his education as quickly as possible. He earned his associate of science degree in forest engineering technology in 1979.

Folwell's training at Lake City covered logging techniques and best management practices, computer programming and operations, firefighting techniques, and using fire as a tool. It also included the management of sixty thousand acres for wildlife, recreation, and the continued growth of the forest, in addition to tree identification, forest measurements, insect and disease management, general safety, and the mechanics of large diesel machinery.

Folwell answered a job posting he saw at the forestry school and soon had his first job with the Georgia Forestry Commission in north Georgia. The job offered him the opportunity to work at various duties, including firefighting and urban forestry. He also interacted with the public about fire prevention and worked with schoolchildren on tree identification during nature hikes. The students nicknamed Folwell the "hug-a-tree guy" because he always ended nature hikes by having them hug a tree.

Job Description

In his present position, Folwell is responsible for shipping and receiving pine pulpwood and saw timber at a company-owned wood yard. Temple Inland Forest manufactures containers and container board, and Folwell works for a district manager who handles more than sixty thousand acres of timberland for harvesting. The timber supplies the paper mill with enough raw materials for the production of paper for the containers.

Folwell's duties are varied, including general management of the wood yard and interacting with about sixty loggers and truckers. One of his staff members has been working in this business for more than twenty years, and Folwell feels that the two of them are a successful team.

What Folwell likes most about his job is the opportunity to interact with other people. He also works well under pressure, which is a helpful quality at those times when twenty-five trucks are in the wood yard and he must keep everything running smoothly. Folwell stresses the importance of safety in the yard, especially when trees are being moved. He works closely with the equipment to ensure that all safety rules are followed. He also enjoys checking on loggers in the woods, since this allows him to spend time in the forest, making sure that the trees are harvested and that all management practices are followed.

All logging comes to a stop when it rains, which is when Folwell does paperwork, the part of the job he likes least.

But overall, Folwell has found forestry to be a very rewarding career. He says, "I am not out for big money or recognition. I like being by myself in the woods. Trees don't hit or hurt or talk back; they just grow. I like to consider myself a person who works closely with nature, and together we can make a strong, healthy forest."

Professional Advice

Folwell recommends that anyone interested in a forestry career gets a good education at a college or technical school. Or, he suggests either contacting paper companies to see whether they are hiring or applying to the state forestry commission or the U.S. Forest Service.

A Range Conservation Career

What better way to learn about the profession than from someone whose career has spanned three decades? Larry Walker earned a B.S. in rangeland science from New Mexico State University in Las Cruces and worked in range conservation until retiring from a long career with the U.S. Department of the Interior, Bureau of Land Management, at the Oregon/Washington state office in Portland, Oregon.

Walker grew up on ranches in northeastern New Mexico. After his sophomore year of high school, he grew restless and joined the navy, where he earned his GED. Following his four-year tour in the navy, he took a variety of jobs, working as a florist, retail clerk, and ranch hand.

It wasn't long before Walker realized that he needed more education. He got a night job as a hotel desk clerk and enrolled in the local New Mexico Highlands University with the intention of getting an associate's degree in electronics, a decision based on finances rather than interest.

Around this time, the G.I. Bill that provides tuition for veterans was amended to include Vietnam veterans, and Walker made a plan. He loved hunting and fishing and learned from friends in the local U.S. Forest Service District that if he worked toward a natural resource degree, he had a good chance of getting a summer job with the Forest Service.

The plan worked, and with what he earned at his summer job and part-time during the school year, combined with a scholarship from a local rancher, a student loan, and his G.I. allowance, Walker was able to finance his college education. His limited finances still dictated the kind of program he could attend because he couldn't afford the tuition to go to an out-of-state school. This ruled out forestry, leaving Walker to choose between range science and wildlife biology to maintain his qualifications for the Forest Service job. Most wildlife jobs at the time were game wardens employed by the state at low salaries. Range conservationist jobs, on the other hand, were with the federal government, which offered much better pay and benefits.

Getting Started

After graduation, Walker was hired by the Bureau of Land Management (BLM) as a GS-7 range conservationist in its Medford District in Oregon. In this position, he administered grazing leases; conducted range studies; and coordinated range, watershed, and wildlife programs with the forestry program. He also coordinated the range program with the Oregon Wildlife Commission; wrote three environmental assessment records; wrote one major fire rehabilitation plan; developed the Deadwood Allotment Coordinated Resource Management Plan in coordination with the Forest Service, timber companies, and range users; updated the range portion of the Unit Resource Analysis (part of BLM's land-use planning system at that time); and developed a number of grazing systems.

After two years on the job, Walker spent the next four working as a natural resource specialist in the Central Oregon Resource Area of BLM's Prineville District. His duties now included conducting watershed evaluations, making public presentations on wild horse claiming procedures, conducting range studies, writing environmental analysis records, and responding to media and public inquiries. Toward the end of this period, he served as acting area manager for several months.

Job Description

For the next twenty years, Walker worked as a range conservationist in BLM's Oregon/Washington state office. Initially he served as the state rangeland resources studies specialist, responsible for coordination, development, training, and direction of soil-vegetation inventories of BLM lands in Oregon and Washington.

Walker also interacted frequently with the staff at BLM's headquarters and at its Denver Service Center, working on the development of inventory methodology for bureauwide application. When the bureau reorganized, placing less emphasis on inventory and more on monitoring, Walker's interaction with the higher levels of the bureau remained the same but he also assumed the duties of Rangeland Program Leader for Budget. In this capacity, he had a substantial involvement in performing program evaluations of management in the rangeland program. He also became Oregon's Noxious Weed and Pesticide Coordinator and was involved in writing and administering contracts. Walker wrote issue papers for the state director as well as responses and reports for numerous inquiries from both the government and the private sector.

About three years before Walker retired, the inception of a new project led to an interesting shift in his duties. The project would require the data from the inventories that had been deemphasized years earlier. His supervisor realized that when Walker retired, he would take with him a huge amount of "institutional memory" and some unique skills that were now valuable to the new project. The supervisor allowed Walker to devote the majority of his time to providing support to the project and documenting as much of the inventory data as he could.

During this period he was able to produce and distribute reports and maps on eastern Oregon's precipitation for the period of 1885 through 1995 and a report and database on Authorized Grazing Within Grazing Districts, 1947–1993. He consolidated Oregon and Washington's rangeland database into a geographic information system and associated relational database, developed a user's guide with documentation of metadata, and presented a workshop on its use the month before he retired.

Looking back on his career, Walker acknowledges that while he was sometimes satisfied and sometimes frustrated, he was seldom bored. He appreciates having had a hand in bringing automation to the BLM and in organizing its rangeland inventory and monitoring procedures.

On the downside, Walker mentions the frequent reorganizations that the bureau underwent, which sometimes led to his work not being acknowledged. He also disliked writing briefing papers for his superiors. Overall, though, he doesn't have any regrets about his career.

Professional Advice

Walker suggests that anyone who wants to work in range conservation should look for temporary summer work during college. This will help you decide if this is the work you really want to do, and it will give you the chance to change majors if it isn't.

He also suggests that once you enter the profession, you should expect to have to change jobs or professions at least five times over the course of your career. In addition, you should take the necessary course work to build a solid foundation in computer-related skills, particularly in the areas of relational databases and geographic information systems.

A Career in the Wild

Stuart Felberg worked for twenty-one years before retiring as an Alaska state trooper in the fish and wildlife division, which falls under the Department of Public Safety. He earned his B.S. in math and industrial technology and his M.S. in biology. He is also a licensed pilot for commercial aircraft, single-engine land and sea aircraft, and helicopters.

Getting Started

Acting on the advice of a friend, Felberg applied to the fish and wildlife division of the Alaska state troopers, hoping to find an interesting job that would provide adventure, the ability to fly, and the chance to protect the wilderness and wildlife.

The minimum qualifications for the job Felberg wanted didn't require any training other than a high school education. Because there were so many applicants for the position he sought, his skills, training, and work history all helped to place him in the forefront of the group of candidates. Patience is an important quality for anyone applying for a state job, because the application process can take considerable time to complete. Felberg had to make numerous phone calls and visit several offices to speak with people about his application, in addition to dealing with administration and personnel offices that conduct preliminary testing and screening prior to accepting an applicant.

Job Description

Working with the Alaska state troopers differs from working in any other state police agency except Oregon. In these two states, the fish and wildlife enforcement division is part of the statewide law enforcement agency instead of being part of the fish and game management and research department. Because of the remoteness of many areas of Alaska and the absence of county and local police forces, state troopers are responsible for statewide law enforcement.

The fish and wildlife trooper serves a dual role, doing traditional police work when necessary as well as enforcing fish and wildlife laws. In Alaska there is significant industry surrounding resource use, such as commercial fishing, the commercial guiding of hunters and fishermen for game and fish, fur trapping, and the utilization of the game and fish resources for subsistence purposes by many groups, including Alaska natives. It is possible that misdemeanor infractions for commercial fishing violations will run into the millions of dollars.

Troopers in Alaska may use an aircraft or a boat for transportation and patrol, may have no highways anywhere near where they work, and may be required to handle problems from barking dogs to rapes and murders to the abuse of children. They are required to do their own investigations, interviews, and evidence gathering and often must present their misdemeanor cases in court, acting as the state's district attorney.

Felberg feels that while public relations is an important part of all police work, it is absolutely essential in Alaska, where taking the time to develop sources of information and trust among the public can benefit a trooper who is working in remote areas with no chance of any backup or assistance from other officers. In Felberg's case, he patrolled a remote area of 160,000 square miles. His patrols were made by small aircraft, boat, snowmobile, and motor vehicle, and often lasted for weeks at a time.

Felberg frequently visited native villages and hunting, fishing, or mining camps, where he would contact individuals and groups to conduct meetings and solicit information. He investigated all complaints and acted as general law enforcement in these areas. He also conducted undercover operations or stakeouts when necessary. In addition, he conducted numerous search and rescue operations as a pilot. These were not all successful, sometimes requiring medical skills beyond his ability or the transport of deceased persons.

Because of the environment in which he worked, Felberg's hours as a state trooper were irregular. The need to catch poachers led to working at night or in bad weather; limited visibility often kept him from flying. Despite this, Felberg loved the diversity and excitement of the job. One day might involve flying in the mountains, looking for a place where someone killed a grizzly bear out of season; the next day might have him operating a skiff in a commercial fishing area; and the next might be spent writing reports and testifying in court.

As a police officer, Felberg was required to respond to emergencies at any time of the day, whether or not he was on duty. In Alaska, emergencies might range from a plane wreck to a motorist stuck on the side of the road at fifty degrees below zero to settling a dispute between angry miners to locating a long overdue dog musher. He occasionally worked months of sixteen-hour days without time off, and on several occasions he worked for up to three straight days.

Felberg found that the work environment varied from people who view police and wildlife officers as their friends and partners in making their world a better place to live, to those who are extremely hostile and view any kind of authority figure as an enemy. Much of the time is spent outdoors, at times in brutal weather conditions.

The work is hard, involving long hours and difficult conditions, and it requires a high degree of dedication. The job also involves considerable risks, whether from violators or from traveling in extreme weather to remote locations.

Felberg acknowledges that it is difficult to maintain a normal home and family life while doing this work, but he says that he can't think of another profession that would have offered him more excitement, freedom, or fulfillment.

The current monthly starting salary for Alaska state troopers ranges from $3,581 to $3,715, depending on location. The minimum base salary after successful completion of probation and promotion to state trooper is $3,999 per month. Felberg reports that in his experience, some of the highest-paid troopers working in the bush eventually earned well over $125,000 per year.

Alaska has withdrawn from the Social Security system, and all funds both from the employee and the employer are put into a fund that accumulates interest throughout one's career. Retirement is available, although not mandatory, after twenty years of service and is about 50 percent of your salary. Along with the funds from the Social Security replacement system, often troopers can retire making more than they did while working. Medical insurance is still paid upon retirement.

Professional Advice

Felberg advises anyone interested in a career as a state trooper to pay particular attention to any skills, education, and work history that would be beneficial in competing with other applicants for the job. Although a college degree is not required, most applicants have a degree and work experience.

Felberg believes that the most important personal attributes necessary for the job are integrity, stability, good judgment, and the ability to interact with people and to maintain a calm state of mind in all situations.

5

HISTORIC LANDSCAPE
PRESERVATION

*There clearly is a desperate need for professionals who are con-
servationists by instinct, but who care not only to preserve but to
create and manage. These persons cannot be impeccable scientists
for such purity would immobilize them. They must be workmen
who are instinctively interested in the physical and biological sciences and who seek this information so that they may obtain the
license to interpose their creative skills upon the land. The landscape architect meets these requirements. He has the precedents of
the 18th century to give him courage . . .*

> —Ian McHarg, *Design with Nature*

ALTHOUGH THESE WORDS were written more than a decade ago,
they still apply today. Historic landscape preservation is a field of
growing interest among managers of historic buildings and cultural
and natural landscapes. Historic landscapes can range from large

tracts of land to a small front yard. They can be designed, formal landscapes or small, cultural landscapes that represent the combined works of nature and of man and illustrate the evolution of human society and settlement over time.

Landscape architects can find work in unique settings, including conducting preservation and renovation planning to initiate design studies at these sites. Locations include Monticello, the home of Thomas Jefferson, and Kykuit, the New York home of John D. Rockefeller. One of the largest and most well-known employers of historic landscape architects, designers, and related groundskeeping professionals is the Colonial Williamsburg Foundation in Williamsburg, Virginia. This chapter will examine some of the careers available at this unique property.

Colonial Williamsburg

Visitors to Colonial Williamsburg meet historical figures, witness events, and participate in the daily lives of the people who helped bring about American independence.

For eighty-one years, from 1699 to 1780, Williamsburg was the thriving capital of Virginia, one of the original thirteen colonies. After the American Revolution, when the state capital was moved to Richmond, Williamsburg began a decline that lasted 146 years. It became a sleepy Southern town with crumbling roads and buildings, overgrown gardens, and only a distant memory of patriots and prosperity.

In 1926, with a love of American history and a belief that anything is possible, John D. Rockefeller Jr. began the Colonial Williamsburg restoration project to return this once-important city to its former glory.

Now, after eighty years of work, more than ninety of the original eighteenth- and early-nineteenth-century structures have been completely restored, and more than five hundred others have been reconstructed on original foundations. Colonial gardens have also been re-created, duplicating the plants used during the eighteenth century. And beautiful three- and four-hundred-year-old trees still stand, lining the hard-packed dirt walkways.

All of this restoration was accomplished only after extensive archaeological and historical investigation.

The Colonial Williamsburg Foundation maintains an informative website where you can search for information about the foundation and the many career opportunities it offers. You can visit www.history.org for details.

A Landscape Architect and Garden Historian at Work

Kent Brinkley is a landscape architect in the Landscape and Facilities Services Department at the Colonial Williamsburg Foundation. He is also a Fellow of the American Society of Landscape Architects, past president of the Virginia chapter, and coauthor with Gordon W. Chappell of the bestselling book *The Gardens of Colonial Williamsburg.*

Brinkley has a bachelor of arts in history from Mary Baldwin College in Staunton, Virginia, and has been employed at Colonial Williamsburg for more than fifteen years.

Getting Started

When asked to describe his start in landscape architecture, Brinkley says that he's "a dying breed." At the time he entered the profession, it was possible to become a landscape architect by working as an apprentice in a landscape architecture office under a licensed practitioner. A graduate with a B.L.A. degree had to spend three years as an apprentice before being able to sit for the licensing exam. As an alternative to the five-year degree program, it was also possible to serve an eight-year apprenticeship and then take the exam.

Brinkley worked as an apprentice for ten years before he took his licensing exam. He started his career as a draftsman and advanced to vice president of the firm before coming to Williamsburg. He describes his job as a perfect combination of his love of history and his work as a landscape architect.

Job Description

Brinkley's job includes several different responsibilities. He creates designs for new work that is being planned and is also responsible for maintaining the existing gardens planted years ago by his predecessors. After extensive research and investigation into the landscapes of colonial times, the gardens at Williamsburg were planted with flowers and plants appropriate to the period. Brinkley makes sure that these plants continue to thrive and selects replacements for any that are no longer healthy. Brinkley works closely with the director of landscape services, providing the design plans that will be implemented by the landscape service staff. He also gives lectures and tours to groups and garden clubs and occasionally conducts public garden tours to keep in touch with the foundation's visitors.

Garden Historian

In addition to his work as a landscape architect, Brinkley is a garden historian. He has a background in history and has conducted research into the development of historical landscapes. He's visited England many times to study country estates and gardens because English landscape design served as the model for many colonial gardens in the eighteenth century.

Brinkley describes garden history as a fairly new field but one that could be a specialty for a landscape architect with an interest in history. Much of his work in this area involves studying what was done historically in gardens, the kinds of plants that were grown, how they were laid out, and the types of fencing that was used, all of which helps him to re-create a period garden.

Landscape Archaeology

Brinkley also works in the growing field of landscape archaeology, in which the goal is to recover enough evidence to re-create a garden that existed on the site in a given historical period. Landscape archaeology uses traditional archaeological technique to recover the fence lines, planting beds, and other evidence.

Brinkley works in conjunction with archaeologists when they excavate a site, the hope being to uncover evidence of the original gardens and to gain information about pathways, fence lines, and postholes, as well as planting beds and outbuilding foundations. Sometimes actual seed materials are found in excavated planting beds, and laboratory analysis can reveal what type of plant the seed is from.

As is the case with gardening history, there is no particular university degree at this time in landscape archaeology. The best route to becoming a landscape archaeologist would be to follow a traditional program in anthropology and archaeology. Then, with a degree and on-the-job experience, you can specialize.

Professional Advice

Based on his own experience, Brinkley offers some insightful advice for aspiring landscape architects. He recommends strengthening your communication skills, because you may have to present your designs to groups of people. Some sales ability is also a plus, because you will have to market not only yourself, but your firm, and the designs as well.

Brinkley stresses that there is a lot of drafting involved in landscape architecture, and he suggests cultivating your drawing talents as a way to develop an edge over the competition for jobs.

He also believes that it's a good idea for anyone entering the field to work for two or three years before taking the licensing exam. Since the exam is comprehensive in scope and tests you on a variety of subjects, having some work experience will help you more than just studying.

Brinkley also suggests that landscape archaeology might be a good specialty for students who are mechanically inclined and curious about how things work.

Finally, he has some encouraging words for up-and-coming landscape architects: "I think there's a bright future in the twenty-first century. For years the architects have beat their chests and said, 'We're the guys who are going to save the world.' But they haven't. They've done some pretty wretched designs. And then the engineers said they could do it, and though they certainly can design functional work, they seem to have no feeling for aesthetics. So, now, there's a growing awareness that landscape architects may be the people to include on the design team. We are the ones who have a broad enough range of expertise to worry about environmental concerns and other things to make the resulting projects user-friendly and earth-friendly."

Landscape Services at Colonial Williamsburg

The Landscape Services Department at Colonial Williamsburg employs about seventy full-time staff members who work year-round maintaining the gardens and landscapes. The general positions within the department are entry-level groundskeeper jobs, followed by a succession of gardener positions. Gardeners progress through three levels (A, B, and C); the highest gardener position is senior gardener. Gardeners are supervised by foremen, who are each responsible for a particular area of the department. Supervisors each manage three or four foremen and report directly to the department director.

The position of groundskeeper is basically an unskilled labor job. The groundskeeper supplies the gardening staff with the brawn to clean up and take care of things. Many groundskeepers have been trained for promotion to gardening positions.

Gardener A is the entry-level position on the gardening ladder and requires a minimum of skills. For instance, an employee in this position would have to know the difference between perennials and annuals and have some general knowledge of pruning and turf maintenance. In addition, some basic knowledge of chemicals, pesticides, herbicides, and fungicides is helpful, even though their use is not required at this level. To be promoted to a gardener B position, a gardener A employee would have to become a certified technician licensed for the use of pesticides by the requirements of the State of Virginia.

Gardener B is a more professional position. Although a college degree isn't required, this gardener must be able to make appropriate calculations for the use of chemicals. Gardener B does all gardening chores and landscape maintenance, watering, pruning, fertilizing, planting, transplanting, bed working, and edging.

Gardener C must have a commercial pesticide license and is responsible for supervising groundskeepers. A gardener at this level must maintain an assigned portion of the landscape.

A senior gardener has similar but more extensive responsibilities than a level C gardener. The senior gardener makes sure that staff gardeners have the materials and equipment they need to do their assigned work and fills in for the foreman if he or she is not available, running the crews and keeping track of employees' time cards.

The foreman oversees a team that takes care of a large geographic area. For example, while a level C gardener may be responsible for seven pieces of property, a foreman might have fifteen or more. A college degree in botany or horticulture is preferred for a foreman position, although it is not required.

Foremen report to the director of landscape services, who is answerable to the director of landscape and facility services. The landscape services director also works closely with the landscape architect and garden historian.

A Lesson in Topiary

Wesley Greene is a landscape supervisor at Colonial Williamsburg who oversees the maintenance of the historic area gardens. He is also a licensed arborist in charge of the tree crew and specializes in topiary.

Greene began working in the industry in high school, taking summer jobs on college campuses, in private industry, and for the National Park Service. He received a bachelor's degree in botany from the University of Maine.

As landscape supervisor, Greene's primary function is to train others and to give technical support to his crew. He oversees the grounds maintenance, supervising twenty-six gardeners and tree surgeons. He does some design and most of the layout for the topiary displays and, because he enjoys it, occasionally does some of the actual topiary work himself.

Greene explains that the word *topiary* comes from the Latin *topiaries,* which means ornamental gardener; it was first used during the Roman era. The art of topiary is the shaping of plants. Although we tend to think of animals or geometric shapes as topiary, in fact any trimmed hedge would qualify.

There are two different kinds of topiary: those formed using wire structures, such as you might see at Disney theme parks, and those formed without wire structures. Greene cites Ladew Gardens in Maryland as one of the best examples of true topiaries formed without wires. The collection at Ladew includes plants shaped like horses and fox hunts. The topiary at Disney parks are designed using wire forms. The plant grows around the form, and gardeners continue to shape it as it grows. Wire forms aren't used at Williamsburg; instead, the plants are allowed to grow into a shape.

Williamsburg has 178 acres of formal gardens, hedges, freestanding pieces, and topiary pieces that are incorporated into hedges. The gardens include *estrade* topiary, which Greene describes as a big gumball shape in a layer cake design with a series of disks. Throughout Williamsburg you'll also see a lot of squares, domes, and circles. Some flattop hedges on the corners will have bubbles on top or diamond shapes, and some hedges sweep up at the corners.

Greene explains that, like the rest of the Williamsburg gardens, the topiary is based on eighteenth-century landscaping. Since animal topiary was considered vulgar by the mid-1700s, there aren't any animal shapes among the gardens.

To train topiary, a gardener shears a plant to get it to the desired shape. It's important to keep a compact plant structure that will withstand the elements, while simultaneously maintaining a straight central trunk. Once the overall shape has been established, the gardeners lay out the design.

Greene employs some algebra in his layouts, believing that there is beauty in mathematics. He offers a saying that he's coined: "Formality by definition is wedded to geometry, and geometry by natural law is insufferable to approximation. That means you're exactly right, or you don't show up."

If you follow a mathematical plan, your eye will naturally pick up the repetition of the design. Greene says that although repetition might sound boring, it's the hallmark of good landscape design; repeating the forms, colors, and shapes throughout the garden design or, with topiary, within the individual piece, is what makes the design successful.

Although it started in the Roman empire, topiary got its real boost much later in Holland, where it was very popular. William and Mary brought it to England, where it was overused to the point that it fell out of favor. A move toward naturalism began in the mid-eighteenth century, when landowners ripped out formal gardens in favor of lakes surrounded by groves of trees.

Experts believe that topiary lasted longer in the United States. This may be partly due to the fact that it held sentimental value, reminding people of what gardens looked like in their home countries. Also, Greene feels that the ability to tame a piece of land in the vast wilderness of the new world might also have added to topiary's appeal. He says, "People are at the mercy of nature, and they respond by trying to control it. It's an insecure way of gardening."

6

Landscape Design and Maintenance

You now know how many years of study are required to become a landscape architect. If you're interested in pursuing this field but don't want to commit to a full course of study, there are other, shorter routes to related careers that provide equally fulfilling work. In this chapter we'll consider the fields of landscape design and maintenance.

Work is available for landscape designers and groundskeepers almost anywhere you see a tree, shrub, or lawn. You probably won't have to search the classified ads or move across the country to find a job. Just look around you at all the possibilities. Each of these settings requires a variety of workers. Here's a list of some places you might consider.

- Arboreta
- Athletic fields
- Botanical gardens

- Cemeteries
- Golf courses
- Highways
- Historic areas
- Hospitals
- Hotels
- Museums
- Office buildings
- Playgrounds
- Private homes
- Public parks and gardens
- Recreational facilities
- Shopping malls
- Theme parks
- University campuses

Landscape Designers

A landscape designer's work is similar to that of a landscape architect but is usually done on residential or small commercial projects. Landscape designers aren't certified and cannot call themselves landscape architects.

Salaries are generally lower for designers than for architects, but those who are self-employed are not as limited as those who work for landscape architecture firms.

Training and Qualifications

You can usually become a landscape designer after completing a two-year associate's degree in a landscape specialist program, which is offered at a number of schools throughout the United States and

Canada. Contact the Association of Professional Landscape Designers for program information; its address is provided in Appendix A. Some botanical gardens, such as Longwood Gardens in Pennsylvania and the New York Botanical Garden, offer certificate programs in landscape design. See Appendix B for a list of botanical gardens.

Most landscape design programs will require that you complete a senior design project. In addition to giving you practical design experience, the senior project can also help you decide on a particular area of design to pursue.

Computer-aided design (CAD) courses are very useful because CAD is used in many areas of design, and most employers will expect you to be familiar with using the computer as a design tool.

Creativity is crucial for landscape designers. You'll need a strong sense of color, an eye for detail, a sense of balance and proportion, sensitivity to beauty, and the ability to communicate ideas both visually and verbally.

Problem-solving skills and the ability to work independently are also important traits. As a landscape designer, you'll need the self-discipline to start projects on your own, budget your time, and meet deadlines. Business sense and sales ability are important if you intend to freelance or run your own business.

Working Conditions and Earnings

Working conditions and places of employment vary. Most designers employed by design firms or nurseries work regular hours in comfortable settings. Self-employed designers tend to work longer hours, especially at first, when they're trying to establish themselves and cannot afford to hire assistants or clerical help.

Landscape designers frequently adjust their work schedule to suit their clients, meeting them in the evenings or on weekends when necessary. They may conduct business in their own offices or in clients' homes or offices.

In addition to their work on outdoor spaces, landscape designers are increasingly finding employment in the interior landscaping business. Most of the work in this area is in large commercial projects for hotels, shopping malls, corporate parks, and similar locations. Interior landscape designers need some additional skills, such as familiarity with interior irrigation systems, seasonal and tropical plants, and the climate conditions necessary for the survival of indoor plants.

All designers face occasional frustration when their designs are rejected or when they can't be as creative as they would like. Independent consultants, who are paid by the assignment, are under pressure to please clients and to find new ones to maintain their incomes.

Earnings can vary depending on the employer, the designer's experience, and the geographic location. In general, landscape designers can expect to earn an annual salary of about $35,000.

A Landscape Designer at Work

Kyle J. Lyssy is a landscape designer with the Garden Center in San Antonio, Texas. He has worked in the field for almost fifteen years and credits his love of the outdoors with spurring his desire to pursue landscape design as a profession. Although he was initially attracted to the field of forestry, it was not an available option because he lives in southwestern Texas. He next considered park management and landscape design and decided that the latter is the better choice in his area.

Getting Started

Lyssy was hired for his current position after applying in person at the company and being interviewed by the owner, who felt that Lyssy's goals and abilities were a good match for a position with the Garden Center. The company is a design/build center, whose main goal is to sell landscape installations. He began at the bottom level, working as a laborer. In this position, Lyssy quickly learned the mechanics of landscape installation and began to desire more responsibility.

A good deal of his training has been from hands-on experience, which he supplemented by reading books on his own time. Lyssy also received direct training from the designer for the Garden Center, as well as from the company's owner, who is a registered landscape architect.

Job Description

As a landscape designer, Lyssy is responsible for a variety of daily duties. He estimates that about 15 percent of his time is spent working on designs, which involves using a CAD system. He meets clients at their homes, creates and presents the design, and sells the job. Once the design is accepted, Lyssy locates and purchases materials and oversees the installation. He also collects payment, follows up with clients, and handles any warranty calls should problems arise after completion of a project.

Lyssy finds his working environment happy and very relaxed because his boss and colleagues all get along well. The atmosphere is pleasant, and his work is usually very interesting. Occasionally, however, it can become a bit boring when clients' requests are all very similar. Lyssy finds that many people have the same basic ideas of how they want their landscapes to look, and his challenge is to try to satisfy their desires while creating a beautiful and unique garden.

Lyssy's workday generally runs from 8:00 A.M. to 5:00 P.M. He sometimes works seven days a week in the spring, but the rest of the year he averages forty-five hours a week over five or six days.

What Lyssy enjoys most about his job is the flexibility allowed by working both indoors and outdoors and not being in one place for any length of time. Every job is different, and he enjoys the opportunity to work with people on a friendly and professional level. He also finds that one of the greatest joys is the immediate gratification he feels when he sees a newly completed landscape.

Lyssy sees as the downsides of his job a fairly limited income, uncontrollable working conditions, and the unwillingness of some clients to commit to a job installation. In addition, employees can cause frustration if their performance is not up to the designer's standards.

Working at the Garden Center, Lyssy is paid a straight commission and earns 10 percent of everything he sells. When he was promoted to designer, he was paid a straight salary with no sales-related bonuses. He later requested a switch to an 8 percent commission and company car but has since found that a 10 percent commission and no car is more profitable.

Professional Advice

Lyssy believes that starting at the bottom is the best way to fully understand all aspects of landscape design. By beginning your career as a laborer and working up from there, you'll experience the various kinds of work that comprise landscape design, and you will be able to decide whether any of these areas are right for you. He also advises that flexibility, creativity, honesty, dependability, and a good ability to communicate effectively will be necessary qualities for anyone to be successful in landscape design.

Gardeners and Groundskeepers

Attractively designed and well-maintained lawns, gardens, trees, and shrubbery create a positive first impression, establish a peaceful mood, and increase property values. Although landscape architects, designers, and related professionals are the ones who develop the designs, it's the gardeners and groundskeepers who implement the plans and maintain the work.

Working Conditions

Many jobs for gardeners and groundskeepers are seasonal, mainly in the spring and summer, when cleanup, planting, mowing, and trimming take place. Gardeners and groundskeepers work outdoors in all kinds of weather and are frequently under pressure to get the job completed, especially when they're preparing for scheduled events, such as athletic competitions or burials.

They work with pesticides, fertilizers, and other chemicals and must exercise safety precautions to prevent exposure. They also work with dangerous equipment and tools such as power lawn mowers, chain saws, and power clippers.

Work Involved

Some landscape gardeners work on large properties, such as office buildings and shopping malls. Following plans drawn up by a landscape architect, they plant trees, hedges, flowering plants, and turf areas and apply mulch for protection.

For residential customers, they install lawns, terrace hillsides, build retaining walls, and install patios, as well as plant flowers, trees, and shrubs. Gardeners working for home owners, estates, and public gardens feed, water, and prune the flowering plants and trees and mow and water the lawn.

Some landscape gardeners, called lawn service workers, specialize in maintaining lawns and shrubs for a fee. A growing number of residential and commercial clients, such as managers of office buildings, shopping malls, multi-unit residential buildings, and hotels and motels favor this full-service landscape maintenance. These workers perform a full range of duties, including mowing, edging, trimming, fertilizing, and mulching.

Those working for chemical lawn service firms are more specialized. They inspect lawns for problems and apply fertilizers, herbicides, pesticides, and other chemicals, as well as practice integrated pest management techniques.

Groundskeepers, often classified as grounds managers or maintenance staff, maintain a variety of facilities including athletic fields, golf courses, cemeteries, university campuses, and parks. Grounds managers usually work at many of the same tasks as maintenance personnel but typically have more extensive knowledge of horticulture, landscape design and construction, pest management, irrigation, and erosion control. In addition, managers usually have supervisory responsibilities.

Groundskeepers who care for athletic fields keep natural and artificial turf fields in top condition and mark out boundaries and paint turf with team logos and names before events. They must make sure the underlying soil on natural turf fields has the proper composition to allow for drainage and support the appropriate grasses used on the field. They regularly mow, water, fertilize, and aerate the fields.

In addition, groundskeepers apply chemicals and fungicides to control weeds, kill pests, and prevent diseases. They also vacuum and disinfect synthetic turf after use to prevent growth of harmful bacteria and periodically remove the turf and replace the cushioning pad.

Groundskeepers in parks and recreation facilities care for lawns, trees, and shrubs; maintain athletic fields and playgrounds; clean buildings; and keep parking lots, picnic areas, and other public spaces free of litter. They may also remove snow and ice from roads and walkways, erect and dismantle snow fences, and maintain swimming pools. These workers inspect buildings and equipment, make needed repairs, and keep everything freshly painted.

Tools of the Trade

Gardeners and groundskeepers use hand tools such as shovels, rakes, pruning saws, saws, hedge and brush trimmers, and axes as well as power lawn mowers, chain saws, snow blowers, and electric clippers.

Some use motorized equipment, including tractors and twin-axle vehicles. Park, school, cemetery, and golf course groundskeepers may use sod cutters to harvest sod that will be replanted elsewhere.

Athletic turf groundskeepers use vacuums and other devices to remove water from athletic fields. In addition, some workers in large operations use spraying and dusting equipment.

Training and Qualifications

There are usually no minimum educational requirements for entry-level positions in grounds maintenance. Most workers have a high school education or less, and a diploma is necessary for some jobs. Short-term on-the-job training is generally sufficient to teach new hires how to operate equipment such as mowers, trimmers, leaf blowers, and small tractors and to follow correct safety procedures.

To work in an entry-level position, you must be able to follow directions, learn proper planting and maintenance procedures, and learn how to repair the equipment you'll be using. If driving is an essential part of the job, your employer will expect you to have a good driving record and some experience driving a truck. Responsibility and self-motivation are also desirable qualities because you may often work with very little supervision. The ability to get along well with people is necessary if you'll be dealing directly with the customers.

Laborers who demonstrate a willingness to work hard and quickly, have good communication skills, and take an interest in the business may advance to crew leader or other supervisory positions. Advancement or entry into positions such as grounds manager and landscape contractor usually requires some formal education beyond the high school level and several years of progressively more responsible experience.

Most states require certification for workers who apply pesticides. Certification requirements vary but usually include passing a test on the proper and safe use and disposal of insecticides, herbicides, and fungicides. Some states require that landscape contractors be licensed.

The Professional Grounds Management Society (PGMS) offers certification to grounds managers who have a combination of eight years of experience and formal education beyond high school and who pass an examination covering subjects such as equipment management, personnel management, environmental issues, turf care, ornamentals, and circulatory systems. The PGMS also offers certification to groundskeepers who have a high school diploma or equivalent, plus two years of experience in the grounds maintenance field.

The Professional Landcare Network (PLANET) offers the designations Certified Landscape Professional (exterior and interior) and Certified Landscape Technician (exterior or interior) to those who meet established education and experience standards and who pass a specific examination. The hands-on test for technicians covers areas such as the operation of maintenance equipment and the installation of plants by reading a plan. A written safety test also is administered. In addition, PLANET offers the designations Certified Turfgrass Professional (CTP) and Certified Ornamental Landscape Professional (COLP), both of which require written exams.

Some workers with groundskeeping backgrounds start their own businesses after several years of experience.

Salaries

According to the most recent available statistics, in 2004 hourly earnings of grounds maintenance workers were as follows:

- First-line supervisors/managers of landscaping, lawn service, and groundskeeping workers—$16.99
- Tree trimmers and pruners—$12.57
- Pesticide handlers, sprayers, and applicators, vegetation—$12.30
- Landscaping and groundskeeping workers—$9.82
- All other grounds maintenance workers—$9.57

The median hourly earnings in the industries employing the largest numbers of landscaping and groundskeeping workers were:

- Elementary and secondary schools—$13.25
- Local government—$11.25
- Services to buildings and dwellings—$9.78
- Other amusement and recreation industries—$9.14
- Employment services—$8.64

Arboriculture

Arboriculture is defined as the preservation and care of trees and shrubs, including woody vines as well as ground cover plantings.

Arborists are the experts who care for trees. They have many responsibilities including planting and transplanting trees, pruning and trimming them, spraying for insects, treating for diseases, fertilizing, bracing, installing lightning protection, and, when necessary, removing them.

Professional arborists also work as consultants. They provide inspections of trees and landscape plants and make reports to insurance companies on tree and other landscape loss due to storm damage, automobile accidents, or vandalism. They can also act as expert witnesses, providing testimony in court cases.

Consulting arborists are qualified to set dollar values for trees for real estate appraisals. During construction of new property, arborists assist in the preservation of existing trees, prepare specifications for planting new trees, and diagnose any problems.

What the Work Involves

For the most part, hands-on tree workers perform jobs that require a great deal of physical labor. They climb trees or work from an aerial lift or a cherry picker, a truck-mounted crane with a large bucket on the end in which the worker stands. They handle heavy and dangerous equipment, such as chain saws, hydraulic pruners, and stump grinders. They work from great heights and haul branches and other cumbersome material.

Arborists also handle pesticides and chemicals for preventive and corrective measures in the treatment of insect problems or diseases. To apply these pesticides, they must be licensed and follow state and federal laws regulating the use of chemicals.

Job Settings

Arborists can work almost anywhere in the country, for a variety of employers.

- **Power companies** hire tree workers to clear tree growth from telephone and power lines.
- **City and county highway departments** employ tree experts to plant and care for trees and shrubs along roadsides.
- **Public parks** require the services of arborists to maintain healthy trees in recreation areas.
- **Arboreta** employ professional arborists to care for their living collections.
- **Private home owners**, condominium complexes, and shopping centers use arborists to plant or remove trees and to treat them for any diseases or insect problems.
- **Landscape contractors** also utilize professional arborists to augment their services.

Training and Qualifications

Requirements vary, but to work as a helper, groundworker, or climber you'll seldom need a formal education; however, a high school diploma is usually desirable. If you hope to advance, you'll need knowledge of additional fields, including arboriculture, biology, botany, entomology, and plant pathology.

Vocational schools and two-year community colleges offer training in this increasingly complex work. On-the-job training is equally important.

If the job description includes the use of pesticides, you must be licensed by a state environmental department. A driver's license, preferably a commercial license for driving trucks and tractors, is also necessary.

The International Society of Arboriculture grants five levels of certification to arborists with experience and education who pass a comprehensive written examination.

Salaries

Just as the duties of arborists vary, so do their salaries. Physical laborers, who generally work the hardest, are paid from $15,000 to $23,000 per year for groundworkers and from $18,000 to $33,000 for climbers. Supervisors or consulting arborists, who rely more on their years of experience and expertise than physical strength, can be paid $45,000 or more.

Job Outlook

Tree care is a promising field. There is a shortage of arborists, possibly because of the low pay and hard work for starting workers. However, more and more home owners, businesses, and cities and towns are recognizing the importance of trees to the environment. A growing commitment to historic preservation and environmental planning also is improving the job market.

Golf Course Management

Golf is the only major sport without a standardized playing field. Every golf course has unique features, from its architecture and design to the different ecosystems and microenvironments found across its acreage. Because of this, golf course managers have to be skilled in a number of disciplines.

Below is a description of the different golf course–related jobs that might appeal to those interested in landscape architecture.

Golf Course Superintendent

The top manager of a golf course assumes a variety of responsibilities. To provide a playing surface that meets aesthetic and playing standards and preserves environmental integrity, he or she must be a scientist familiar with agronomy, entomology, soil science, meteorology, chemistry, physics, and more.

The superintendent is responsible for the maintenance, operation, and management of the golf course. General responsibilities include supervising the construction and maintenance of the course, which covers the golf course itself, clubhouse grounds and landscaping, any other acreage around the course, tennis courts, and a sod farm and nursery, if applicable.

Assistant Golf Course Superintendent

The assistant golf course superintendent reports directly to the superintendent, directing and participating in the maintenance of tees, greens, fairways, and cart paths. In this capacity, an assistant superintendent must be knowledgeable about seeding, planting, cultivating, and pruning plants, shrubs, and trees. Additional responsibilities include the proper use of fertilizers and pesticides, drainage control methods, and irrigation systems.

Horticulturist

The horticulturist manages the greenhouse and nursery, selecting, propagating, and growing plant materials for the ornamental landscaping of the golf course and clubhouse. The horticulturist designs flower beds, trims and prunes shrubs, applies fertilizers and pesticides, designs and maintains irrigation systems, and supervises the groundskeeping staff.

Irrigation Specialist

The irrigation specialist is responsible for programming, operating, and maintaining the golf course irrigation systems. This includes seeding and watering greens, tees, and fairways; laying sod; and repairing greens.

Chemical Technician

The chemical technician, supervised by the superintendent or assistant superintendent, performs chemical applications on golf course properties. This includes fertilizing tees, greens, and fairways; applying chemicals as needed; and preparing preliminary reports on pesticide usage for the superintendent.

Gardener-Triplex Operator

The gardener-triplex operator uses light motorized equipment to mow greens, tees, and aprons, and rakes sand traps with power rakes. Other responsibilities include aerating and spiking greens and operating the sod cutter and fertilizer spreaders.

Greenskeepers

Workers who maintain golf courses are called greenskeepers. They perform many of the same tasks as other groundskeepers, providing routine manual labor to keep the course maintained. Typical responsibilities include operating mowers and string trimmers, cleaning flower beds, and watering and fertilizing the grounds. In addition, the greenskeeper often assists with projects such as construction of new greens and installation of new walkways and paths.

Training and Education

The requirements for a career at a golf course are as varied as the number of positions needed to keep a course running smoothly. A groundskeeper relies on physical strength and the ability to follow directions, while a horticulturist or superintendent must have a specific level of education and experience.

For a career as a golf course superintendent, your best choice would be an undergraduate degree in agronomy, turfgrass management, crop science, horticulture, or a related science with emphasis in turfgrass management. If you have a bachelor's degree in an unrelated field, you can pursue an associate or certificate program at a number of schools. You'll also need strong administrative ability and excellent oral and written communication skills.

Continuing education and certification are important steps toward career advancement for golf course superintendents. The Golf Course Superintendents Association of America offers certification for qualified members who seek this opportunity. An applicant for certification must have a specified level of education and experience and must pass a six-hour written examination.

In most cases, a career as a horticulturist at a golf course requires an associate's degree or extensive experience in horticulture or a closely related field. The irrigation specialist and chemical technician positions do not have any established educational criteria, but to apply for these jobs, you should have experience in the field and need to be a licensed pesticide applicator.

Cemetery Workers

Cemetery workers prepare graves and maintain cemetery grounds. They dig graves to a specified depth, generally using a backhoe, and may place concrete slabs on the bottom and around the sides of the grave to line it for greater support. When readying a site for a burial ceremony, they position the casket-lowering device over the grave, cover the immediate area with an artificial grass carpet, erect a canopy, and arrange folding chairs to accommodate mourners.

Cemetery workers regularly mow grass, apply fertilizers and other chemicals, prune shrubs and trees, plant flowers, and remove debris from graves. They also must periodically build the ground up around new grave sites to compensate for settling.

Cooperative Extension Service

In the early 1900s the United States was largely an agrarian society, and farmers felt they needed more information about agriculture in order to do a better job feeding the nation. At that time, approximately 40 percent of the population was spread out in rural areas, and the rest resided in urban centers. (The proportions have since changed, with only about 3 or 4 percent living in agricultural areas and rural settings.)

At the time, a number of issues to help the nation's agricultural interests were brought before Congress. First, a bill was passed forming land-grant colleges so that every state would have a college that would be technical in nature, with its main focus to conduct research in agriculture.

Second, Congress recognized the need for physical locations in which to conduct related research. Because field rather than laboratory research was required, research stations associated with each land-grant college were established. They were located at the universities, or nearby, wherever the crops were. In some states, more than one research station was established.

Third, Congress realized that all of this new research and the resulting knowledge had to be disseminated to those who needed it. This is how the Cooperative Extension Service was born.

The title *cooperative* was chosen because the program is funded with state, county, and federal monies. Every county has at least one, if not more, programs. There is an advisory board for each county that points out areas that need to be addressed and services that need to be offered.

Although the name has been changed to the Cooperative State Research, Education, and Extension Service to better reflect the agency's goals, local county offices are still called Cooperative Extension Service locations.

What the Cooperative Extension Service Does

The function of the Cooperative State Research, Education, and Extension Service (CSREES) has expanded beyond agricultural issues and now also covers home economics, the 4-H youth program, and a program that helps commercial fishermen.

CSREES works with the community and tries to bring the research that's done at the universities to the public where it's needed. To accomplish this, CSREES employs professional horticulturists and educators as Cooperative Extension agents.

Close-Up Look at a Cooperative Extension Service Office

The Palm Beach County Cooperative Extension office is a branch of the University of Florida's Institute of Food and Agricultural Sciences. As such, the extension office helps to apply the results of research from the university to solve agricultural problems.

The extension office functions as part of a publicly funded educational network that consists of federal, state, and local partners. The office's services are available to home owners, farmers, builders, small-business owners, students, and the general public.

The office provides assistance and education in various areas of agriculture. For example, environmental horticulture issues include selection and placement of plants for energy and water conservation, mulching and composting practices that reduce and recycle trash, commercial nursery production and marketing, and the use of plants to attract wildlife. For family and consumer sciences, the extension office provides information about food safety, food and nutrition education, and hurricane or disaster preparation.

There is also a strong 4-H/youth development program that includes more than fifty projects, including citizenship, marine science, animal and pet care, leadership training, life skills, and organizing various school and 4-H clubs. The Agricultural Economic Development Program works to enhance agricultural opportunities in the country, promote job growth, and identify and develop new products and markets.

The extension office is open for questions from the public on weekdays from 9:00 A.M. to 5:00 P.M. Trained staff and volunteers answer all sorts of questions about plants, pesticides, and environmental issues. Since Palm Beach County is more urban than agricultural, most of the office's work involves urban horticulture. The county has a high number of commercial nursery and landscaping businesses that also require the office's assistance with crop and plant problems. The office provides publications on topics such as lawns and landscapes; livestock, pets, fish, and wildlife; agribusiness and community development; and soil and water.

Becoming a Cooperative Extension Agent

A cooperative extension agent is an employee of the land-grant college and the county. The position requires a master's degree in whatever field is appropriate, for example, vegetable science, entomology, pathology, or any related subjects. The Palm Beach County office has agents with degrees in fruit crops, plant protection, education, and biology. Some counties have affiliated positions called *county agents,* which require a bachelor's degree.

More and more extension offices are becoming involved with policy-related issues, so there is a growing need for agents who can work with the community on environmental issues. In these positions, a degree in sociology or pubic health could also be applicable. In any case, the needs of the specific county determine what services the extension office will provide. For example, extension agents in Maine will not have the same expertise as agents in New Mexico.

Every office also has a director to whom the extension agents report. To become a director, a master's degree is required as well as several years of experience working as an extension agent. The willingness to work hard is also a requirement, since agents are always on call. Particularly in areas prone to natural disasters such as hurricanes or tornadoes, extension agents are relied on to provide advice and to help residents prepare for an emergency and deal with its aftermath.

Salaries for Extension Agents

Salaries follow state and county scales and vary from region to region. A bachelor's level affiliated agent could expect a starting salary of around $30,000. A new agent just out of graduate school could earn close to $40,000, and experienced agents can earn more than $50,000.

Finding a Job with CSREES

CSREES has a national office in Washington, DC, and maintains a national job bank that is available online. The site provides links to the land-grant colleges offering positions. Jobs are also posted at the schools themselves, as well as at individual extension offices. You can contact the schools directly; land-grant colleges are usually part of the state university system. Contact information for CSREES is given in Appendix A.

If you are serious about pursuing a career with CSREES, it's a good idea to be prepared to relocate. Decide where in the country you'd like to work, making sure that you're familiar with the different horticultural requirements for that area; then call the various land-grant colleges for job openings, or check the CSREES website for available positions.

In addition, there are five land-grant colleges outside the United States: American Samoa Community College, University of Guam, College of Micronesia-Kolonia, Northern Marianas College, and University of the Virgin Islands.

Canadian Agricultural Services

Canada does not have a Cooperative Extension Service, but it does have AgriWeb Canada, a service provided by Agriculture and Agri-Food Canada, part of the Department of Agriculture.

The mission of Agriculture and Agri-Food Canada (AAFC) is to provide information, research and technology, and policies and programs to ensure the security of the nation's food system and the health of the environment. It is also a means of promoting innovation and growth in Canadian agriculture.

AgriWeb Canada is a national directory of agricultural resources available via the Internet and other electronic means. Users can search AgriWeb Canada for resources by keyword, subject, author, or geographic regions. They can also browse the complete list of resources, presented in alphabetical order. Farmers, scientists, government officials, and the general pubic are all users of this resource.

AgriWeb Canada provides online resources about Canadian agriculture produced in Canada or produced by a Canadian organization. It doesn't include information intended to promote a company or sell products or services; it is intended to be used as an informational tool.

For more information about Canadian agricultural resources and a link to AgriWeb Canada, contact Agriculture and Agri-Food Canada. Its address is listed in Appendix A.

Job Outlook for Landscape Design and Maintenance

If you're interested in a career in landscape design or grounds maintenance, you should find plentiful job opportunities over the next several years. Demand for these services is growing, and because wages for beginners are low and the work is physically demanding, many employers have difficulty attracting enough workers to fill all openings. These fields also have a high turnover rate, which should contribute to the number of job openings, including at the supervisory and managerial level.

More workers should be needed to keep up with increasing demand by lawn care and landscaping companies, and employment of grounds maintenance workers is expected to increase up to 27 percent through the year 2014.

Anticipated growth in the construction of all types of buildings, from office buildings to shopping malls and residential housing, plus more highways and parks, should increase demand for landscape designers and grounds maintenance workers. The upkeep and renovation of existing landscaping and grounds are also continuing sources of employment. More and more owners of many buildings and facilities recognize the importance of "curb appeal" in attracting business and maintaining the value of the property, and they are expected to use grounds maintenance services more extensively to maintain and upgrade their properties.

Home owners are also a growing source of demand for landscape designers and grounds maintenance workers, as many people realize that a well-designed and maintained landscape is not only attractive, it also adds considerably to the value of a home. Many two-income households lack the time to take care of their property, so they are increasingly hiring people to maintain it for them. Home owners are also showing greater interest in their backyards, as well as a desire to make the yards more attractive for outdoor entertaining. With many newer homes having more and bigger windows overlooking the yard, it becomes important to maintain and beautify the grounds. Also, as the population ages, more elderly home owners will require lawn care services to help maintain their properties.

Job opportunities for tree trimmers and pruners should increase as utility companies step up pruning trees around electric lines to prevent power outages. Additionally, these workers will be needed to help combat infestations caused by new species of insects from other countries. Ash trees in Michigan, for example, have been especially hurt by a pest from China.

Job opportunities for nonseasonal work are more numerous in regions with temperate climates, where landscaping and lawn services are required all year. However, opportunities may vary with local economic conditions.

Growth in the number of parks, athletic fields, golf courses, cemeteries, and similar facilities also can be expected to add to the demand for these workers.

Employment opportunities in landscaping are tied to local economic conditions. During economic downturns, many workers turn to landscaping as a second source of income or a new career. At the same time, demand for landscaping services often slows as corporations, governments, and home owners reduce spending on all nonessential expenditures, increasing the level of competition for available jobs. In addition, state and local governments may face budget cuts, which can affect hiring.

PART TWO

Botanical Gardens and Arboreta

7

CAREERS IN BOTANICAL GARDENS AND ARBORETA

BOTANICAL GARDENS AND arboreta are parks that are open to the general public, students, and research scientists. Plants, flowers, trees, and shrubs are collected from all over the world and exhibited in arrangements by family, country of origin, or with regard to aesthetics.

Typical visitors to botanical gardens and arboreta generally fall into six categories: dedicated professional scientists and horticulturists who utilize the gardens' collections for research purposes or to identify specific plants; professional and amateur gardeners who participate in adult education classes and training programs; horticultural students enrolled in internship programs through their universities; local residents who come to enjoy a peaceful sanctuary; schoolchildren and their teachers; and international travelers and scientists interested in the collections and history of the gardens.

Functions of Botanical Gardens and Arboreta

Public botanical gardens and arboreta play an important role in horticultural education. Through the design, interpretation, and management of a variety of collections of plants, trees, and shrubs, botanical gardens and arboreta perform the following functions:

- **Public programs.** Botanical gardens and arboreta generally offer public programs such as classes in gardening, question-and-answer hotlines to help with gardening problems, tours of the grounds, and lectures on the various collections. These programs help to teach people how to care for their plants, add to their knowledge of unusual or new plants, and help foster an understanding of and appreciation for landscape design.
- **Research.** Most botanical gardens and arboreta are involved with ongoing research issues. Curators and other horticulturists go on collection trips to add to the types of plants in their gardens and to study the plant life in other geographic regions. Living plants are added to the grounds, and pressed and dried plants are stored in herbaria and are shared with researchers all over the world. Through these activities, garden professionals are able to save rare and endangered plants by studying their requirements and offering a protected environment while reintroducing them to the wild.
- **Introduction of new plants.** Public gardens play a role in introducing new plants to the nursery and home landscaping markets through plant collecting, selection, and breeding.
- **Beautification.** Public gardens provide a tranquil setting in the midst of busy cities for walkers and nature lovers.
- **Preservation.** Historic gardens are preserved and interpreted to the public through the use of slides, films, lectures, brochures, and labels.

• **Conservation education.** Public gardens help both children and adults to develop an appreciation for gardening and to be concerned about protecting the natural environment.

• **Community improvement.** Public gardens participate in city beautification projects through plant breeding and selection.

Job Titles

Keep in mind that job titles can vary from institution to institution. Table 7.1 describes the responsibilities associated with key positions in botanical gardens and arboreta. Figure 7.1 on pages 108–109 shows some of the different career paths in botanical gardens and arboreta.

A Professional at Work

Thomas P. Mishler worked for several years as the executive director of the Awbury Arboretum Association in Philadelphia, Pennsylvania. He earned his B.A. in Spanish language and literature with a minor in business administration from Eastern Michigan University and went on to earn his masters in landscape architecture and regional planning with an urban design specialization at the University of Michigan.

Getting Started

Mishler was initially attracted to landscape architecture by its combination of practical problem solving and design. He's always enjoyed plants and trees and has early memories of growing things as a child.

Table 7.1 Key Positions in Botanical Gardens and Arboreta

Administration, Facilities, Security

Position	Job Description
Director	Provides leadership and is responsible for policy making, funding, planning, organizing, staffing, and directing activities throughout the institution.
Assistant Director	Has general responsibility for operations, which may include finance, personnel, and maintenance of facilities, security, and safety.
Business Manager	Is responsible for accounting, payroll and benefits, purchasing, personnel, and financial record keeping.
Store Manager	Manages the institution's gift shop or store.
Security Officer	Guards property against theft, illegal entry, fire, and vandalism. Enforces rules and regulations, protects visitors, and may be required to administer first aid.

Horticulture and Curation of Collections

Head of Horticulture	Directs the horticultural function of the institution, including the management of staff, programs, activities, and plant collections.
Curator of Horticulture	Advises on plant care and acquisitions.
Plant Records Keeper	Maintains inventory of plants. Processes acquisitions, accession and deaccession, mapping, relocating, and labeling.
Horticultural Production Supervisor	Supervises the growing of plants in the nursery.
Propagator	Propagates plant materials for collections.

Grounds Management

Horticulture Supervisor	Supervises garden workers, plans and schedules work assignments.
Foreman	Directs laborer crews in general groundskeeping tasks.
Laborer	Maintains general grounds.
Gardener	Is responsible for the maintenance of a specialized plant area or collection.
Arborist	Is responsible for the care of trees, including trimming, transplanting, and removing.

Education, Visitor Services

Position	Job Description
Head of Education	Responsible for several departments or programs. Supervises several education professionals and/or volunteers.
Education Specialist	Responsible for a specific program. Supervises staff related to that program.
Visitor Services Manager	Coordinates informational programs and services.

Early in his career, Mishler worked for a Fort Lauderdale firm that had many design projects in the Caribbean, including master planning resorts and golf course communities. He next worked for a company that handled urban design projects. While he found these projects challenging and satisfying, Mishler became frustrated by not seeing the fruits of his labors. City planning is interesting, but the plans are for the future, and he rarely got to see a project completed. He also became uncomfortable with his role as a site planner for more and more suburban subdivisions that often turned historic open spaces into tract housing developments.

In Mishler's opinion, no matter how nice the design of a subdivision was, it destroyed the landscape forever. This particularly bothered him because he entered the profession hoping to preserve land. He later worked with the Pennsylvania Horticultural Society, where he was able to reclaim urban wastelands and then work with community-based development groups to plan and restore the vacant land in their neighborhoods. This was much closer than urban development to his ideal practice of landscape architecture.

Mishler also spent a year as a volunteer with an organization that serves the homeless in Philadelphia. He then worked for four years at the Pennsylvania Horticultural Society's Philadelphia Green Program, which works with inner city communities, turning vacant lots into community green spaces.

Figure 7.1 Sample Horticulture Department Organization Chart

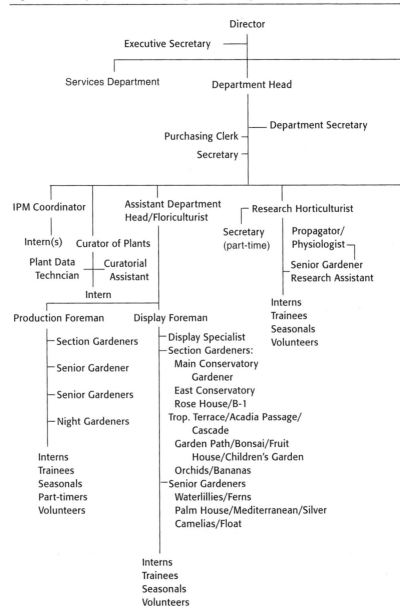

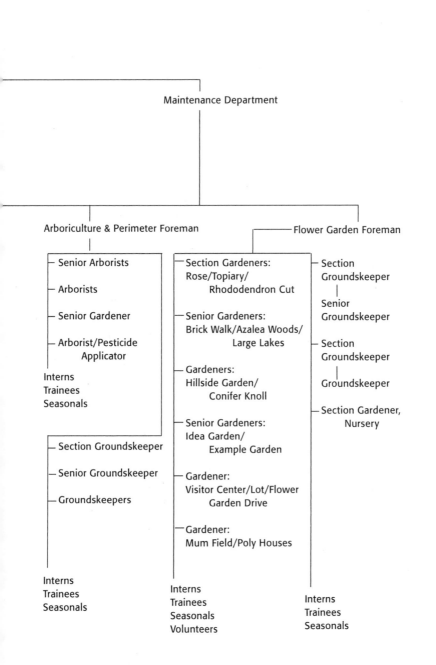

Maintenance Department

Arboriculture & Perimeter Foreman

- Senior Arborists
- Arborists
- Senior Gardener
- Arborist/Pesticide
  Applicator

Interns
Trainees
Seasonals

- Section Groundskeeper
- Senior Groundskeeper
- Groundskeepers

Interns
Trainees
Seasonals

- Section Gardeners:
  Rose/Topiary/
    Rhododendron Cut

- Senior Gardeners:
  Brick Walk/Azalea Woods/
    Large Lakes

- Gardeners:
  Hillside Garden/
    Conifer Knoll

- Senior Gardeners:
  Idea Garden/
    Example Garden

- Gardener:
  Visitor Center/Lot/Flower
    Garden Drive

- Gardener:
  Mum Field/Poly Houses

Interns
Trainees
Seasonals
Volunteers

Flower Garden Foreman

- Section
  Groundskeeper
  |
  Senior
  Groundskeeper

- Section
  Groundskeeper
  |
  Groundskeeper

- Section Gardener,
  Nursery

Interns
Trainees
Seasonals

Landing the Job

Mishler first learned of the job at Awbury Arboretum while attending a seminar on open space issues. He applied for the position—despite thinking that the salary was rather low—and made such a good impression that he was the only person to go through the interview process. His first interview was on a walk of the grounds with the president following an ice storm, when the fifty-acre gardens were frozen and dangerous to navigate. But Mishler was too interested in the job to let some ice stop him. He started working as executive director six months after that first interview.

Job Description

Mishler describes the job as having been fairly busy most of the time. As executive director, he worked with the board to set policy and make plans for the future. He also served as project manager for the Comprehensive Master Plan. His staff of seven handled various aspects of the arboretum's operations.

Fund-raising is a major and ongoing part of the director's job, and Mishler spent a great deal of time planning and writing major grant applications. Another important responsibility is the budget, for which he worked with each manager to develop a budget for his or her particular area. This involved a lot of teamwork, including working closely with the treasurer, and the budget had to be presented to the board for review and approval.

Mishler also prepared an annual report that summarized the major events and accomplishments of the previous year. He frequently represented the arboretum at special events and with other cultural organizations. He also made presentations to local civic groups and garden clubs, occasionally leading tours of the arboretum grounds and historic house.

Although moving from design to management was a difficult decision, Mishler found that he enjoyed the variety of the directorship. The position allowed him to meet many interesting people, and he preferred master planning an entire organization to a single site.

The other part of the job that he thoroughly enjoyed was helping people. Awbury Arboretum offers job training for disadvantaged adults who might have difficulty finding employment. It also provides educational enrichment for thousands of students from inner city schools, and the arboretum is often the first encounter with nature for these children. Mishler sees this as an opportunity to have a real impact on their lives and perhaps even to influence their future career decisions.

One of the things he liked least about the job was the constant focus on money. He also disliked having to pacify or cater to board members who felt their own needs should be addressed before those of the organization. In addition, having to occasionally fire an employee wasn't something he enjoyed.

Salary

Mishler earned $47,500 per year, which represents the median salary for small cultural organizations in the Delaware Valley. His income is supplemented by personal investments.

Mishler feels that although salaries in the nonprofit sector are often much lower than those in the profit sector, the opportunity to do good work is part of the reward. However, the nonprofit sector is becoming increasingly competitive, especially for people who have demonstrated success in fund-raising and leadership. Mishler sees many opportunities to work for organizations that are trying to save open space, protect biodiversity, help disadvantaged persons, or any number of excellent causes that would benefit from the skills landscape architects can bring to the table.

Professional Advice

Mishler advises that working in the nonprofit sector is not for everyone. Money shouldn't be the major motivating factor for these careers, because there just isn't that much available for cultural institutions and nonprofits.

"I would strongly urge people to follow their hearts," he says. Mishler suggests doing some volunteer work first to see if the field still appeals to you. He says you'll meet interesting people and make important connections, as he unexpectedly did through his work with the homeless.

Mishler also says, "Working for the nonprofit sector does not mean meeting a lower threshold of professionalism. I believe it is essential to do your best work, no matter where you are. If you are volunteering your services, do so with all your attention and care. It will pay off in the long run. Don't give in to the temptation to do a second rate job because it is free. On that same note, I think it best not to give away your work. It is better to offer it at a deep discount but still charge something."

8

TRAINING FOR CAREERS IN BOTANICAL GARDENS AND ARBORETA

THE TRAINING OPTIONS for careers in botanical gardens and arboreta are as varied as the many job titles found there. Qualifications needed run the gamut from a high school diploma with special skills to a full-fledged Ph.D. scientist. All workers must, of course, have an interest and some background in horticulture.

Education Requirements

The following is a look at selected career areas and the education requirements for each.

Groundskeepers

As Chapter 6 showed, groundskeepers find work in a variety of settings, including botanical gardens and arboreta. This is a field where there are no minimum education requirements for entry-level jobs, and advancement occurs with on-the-job training and hands-on experience.

Horticulturists

Horticulturists have a variety of backgrounds, from extensive hands-on experience to formal university degrees. Those employed in botanical gardens and arboreta generally have a master's degree in plant sciences or related fields, as well as experience working in horticultural settings.

Curators

Positions as curators, including entry-level assistant curator positions, generally require a minimum of a bachelor's degree in plant sciences or related disciplines. Curators come into their jobs from a variety of backgrounds. Some work their way up through the ranks, some come in from university settings, and others move in from related settings, such as retail horticulture.

Department Heads

The more administrative the position, the more written and oral communication skills are needed, along with degrees and previous experience. Again, many department heads are promoted from within curator or related positions. A bachelor's degree in business, or in plant sciences with additional administrative experience, would be the minimum requirement for entry into this field. A master's degree is increasingly becoming the norm for a position as department head.

Education Professionals

Most professionals involved with outreach work, visitor services, and education-related positions within botanical gardens have at least a bachelor's degree; many have master's degrees. In addition to a knowledge of horticulture, other necessary skills for the job include excellent written and verbal abilities and people skills.

Research Scientists

Research and plant scientists usually have at least a master's degree, and most have earned a doctorate in their field of study.

Internships

If you ask botanical garden or arboretum professionals what kind of training they think you'll need, they're all likely to recommend a college internship as a way to get started. Not only will an internship provide you with contacts for future employment, it will expose you to the different career options available within these settings and help you define the training path you'll need to follow.

Horticulture is a profession that requires work experience and on-the-job training in addition to education. Most employers say they would not hire anyone without work experience, whether it involves summer jobs or an internship program.

Internship Focus

Most public gardens offer one or more student internship programs, though they might differ in the degree of responsibility and the departments in which the intern could work.

Longwood Gardens in Pennsylvania is a well-known botanical garden with a highly regarded internship program. Interns at Longwood gain direct gardening experience, learning the skills, equipment, methods, and procedures used in public display facilities. Internships are offered for both high school and college students, although the high school program is limited to students from certain local schools.

College internships at Longwood Gardens are available in the following areas:

- Arboriculture
- Continuing education
- Curatorial
- Display design
- Greenhouse production
- Groundskeeping
- Horticulture indoor display
- Horticulture research
- Integrated pest management
- Library·science
- Marketing
- Nursery
- Outdoor display
- Performing arts
- Planning and design

- Student programs
- Visitor education

Internship Details

Internships can run from three months to a year, and each intern selects one area of specialization to study. The program is open to current college students and to those who have graduated within the past year and are legally able to work in the United States.

The International Gardener Training Program is available to international students.

In 2006, interns received a taxable stipend of $7.50 per hour. They typically work a seven-hour shift four days a week and spend one half-day on learning activities, including lectures and field trips. Occasional weekend, evening, and holiday work may also be required. Student housing is available.

Some gardens offer professional gardener programs. Longwood's program is a two-year stint combining academics and hands-on training.

Longwood Garden's Professional Gardener Training Program

This tuition-free two-year internship program is offered every other year and is open to those with a high school diploma and at least one year of experience in garden work. Students work three days a week in all horticultural areas of the garden and receive classroom instruction from Longwood staff and outside instructors two days per week. They also rotate as the supervisor of a student work crew, which helps develop people management skills. As in the college internship program, students receive a stipend of $7.50 per hour, and housing is available.

Students work at one-month work rotations in each of eight major indoor and outdoor areas at Longwood—arboriculture, indoor display, production, groundskeeping, outdoor display, research, integrated pest management, and curatorial.

Graduates of the Professional Gardener Training Program are sought after by employers such as public gardens, commercial horticulture companies, and estate gardens. Internships are competitive; only sixteen students at a time are accepted into this program.

Finding an Internship

To find the internship or professional gardener program that's right for you, contact the garden of your choice directly or go through your university department's internship office.

There is also a directory of more than five hundred internships and summer programs published by the American Public Gardens Association. Its address is in Appendix A. The addresses of selected botanical gardens and arboreta are listed in Appendix B.

A Student Intern's Experience

Anne Brennan graduated from Penn State with a bachelor of science in horticulture and worked at Longwood Gardens as a postgraduate intern in the education division. It was a ten-month paid internship, providing a monthly stipend and free housing. Here are her recollections about her time at Longwood.

Brennan initially considered horticultural production in a greenhouse or nursery as a possible career. However, she realized that there are so many other options than just growing plants, an observation that was reinforced during her internship, when she saw new opportunities every day.

Since botanical gardens weren't emphasized in her college studies, Brennan was unaware of the career possibilities that exist for horticulturists, educators, publicists, groundskeepers, and many other professionals. She observes that this gap in her undergraduate education might be the result of her school's curriculum and teachers who focus on research and academics rather than practical experience and production. Although her advisor frequently suggested graduate school, she wasn't very excited by the idea. Once she graduated and began her internship at Longwood, Brennan saw many other options that better suited her.

She worked in the student programs office at Longwood Gardens. This is the office that coordinates the internship programs, including the professional gardener training program and the international student internship program. In effect, Brennan worked as an intern coordinating other interns.

Brennan's internship included working on various projects that she found interesting. She responded to questions from students interested in the programs. She also helped with rewriting the promotional materials on the programs and organized the orientation program for the new interns. In this capacity, Brennan arranged for speakers to address the students, led tours of the grounds, and organized field trips to other botanical gardens.

Good communication skills were an important part of Brennan's job because she interacted regularly with forty students in the different areas of the gardens. She attended meetings twice a month and wrote a long weekly memo that served as a newsletter to keep students informed about upcoming activities. Brennan was the first person visitors met when they came to the student programs office, and she enjoyed meeting new people. She also learned some management skills by running meetings.

Although uncertain about her future plans, Brennan expressed interest in garden writing and education. She has some experience working for a horticultural trade magazine and is eager to learn publishing and layout. She is also considering pursuing a full-time career in the education program of a public garden.

In the next chapter, you will learn about several different career positions in botanical gardens and arboreta from firsthand accounts of people working in the field.

9

FIRSTHAND ACCOUNTS

WHAT BETTER WAY to learn about a profession than from someone with direct experience in the field? The firsthand accounts you'll read in this chapter cover the following careers in botanical gardens and arboreta:

- Curator
- Curatorial associate
- Outreach horticulturist
- Senior biologist
- Horticulturist

Curator of Plants, Longwood Gardens

Rick Darke served on the staff of Longwood Gardens for twenty years—eleven as curator of plants. He has a bachelor's degree in plant sciences from the University of Delaware, and he also studied art and anthropology before deciding on his major.

His first job was as an intern at Longwood Gardens, and he later moved up to assistant taxonomist (taxonomy is the science of classifying living things). He took some graduate courses but ended up having the opportunity to take over a doctoral position in taxonomy that was rewritten as curator of plants. When the man Darke worked for announced that he would retire in two years, Darke had to choose between continuing in a graduate program or staying on the job and developing the skills he'd need to take over the position. He chose to stay, and it was a good decision.

One of Darke's main responsibilities as curator of plants was to oversee the identification, mapping, and labeling of plants done by the curatorial assistants working under his supervision. Identifying and labeling every item grown at Longwood Gardens is one of the most important tasks.

Darke participated regularly on landscape and advisory committees, making recommendations and working with teams of colleagues to create and restore the gardens. His role was to suggest plants that could be used in place of existing plantings or to comment on architectural details or other design elements.

As a curator, Darke traveled extensively while working at Longwood. He visited Australia, New Zealand, Japan, South Africa, Brazil, England, and Germany, bringing plants from different climates back from each trip. Longwood Gardens includes a four-acre area under glass where the staff can create specialized environments for plants from other climates.

Darke's duties included a considerable amount of teaching. Longwood Gardens offers several student programs, and Darke regularly taught a botany course in the Professional Gardener Training Program, and other classes for graduate students. He also taught courses for the continuing education program, including evening lectures and field trips, and led tours to native areas and other gardens.

Darke is also a writer. He contributed to the Longwood Gardens in-house publication and wrote magazine articles about happenings at Longwood. For example, he traveled to Brazil and worked with a landscape architect there whom he brought back to Pennsylvania. The architect created a garden at Longwood, and Darke wrote an article about it, collaborating with a photographer to publish a celebration of the gardens at Longwood.

Darke most enjoyed the eclectic mix of his job and the interaction he had with students. There was usually an intern working in his office, and he was also always regularly teaching people as they moved through the organization. Over the years, he made a strong network of friends and professional colleagues across the country and throughout the world.

Since leaving Longwood Gardens, Darke has served as a horticultural consultant for public gardens and landscapes. His clients include the Chicago Botanic Garden, the Rio Grande Botanic Garden, and Baltimore's Druid Hill Conservatory. He lectures nationally on topics related to horticulture and landscape architecture and is an active freelance writer and photographer. His books include *The American Woodland Garden: Capturing the Spirit of the Deciduous Forest* (Timber Press) and *The Color Encyclopedia of Ornamental Grasses* (Timber Press).

Professional Advice

Darke says that to succeed as a curator of plants, you'll need certain skills in addition to your love of plants. Strong writing and verbal skills are very important because you'll interact with many different people. He stresses that he would not have been able to do his job well without the ability to communicate clearly and to teach others.

Curatorial Associate, Arnold Arboretum

The Arnold Arboretum is located in Jamaica Plain, Massachusetts, a section of Boston, and is affiliated with Harvard University. Its mission is the biology, cultivation, and conservation of temperate woody plants.

The Arnold Arboretum was established in 1874 by Harvard botanist Asa Gray. It began with 123 species of neglected woody plants and has grown to include 265 beautifully maintained acres, with approximately fifteen thousand plants in its living collection.

Susan Kelley is a curatorial associate for the arboretum's living collections. Her job involves mapping the living specimens on the grounds and labeling each plant. Kelley earned bachelor's and master's degrees in music before deciding to change careers. She earned a master's in plant population from City University of New York and then worked at the Harvard University Herbaria until she applied for her position at Arnold Arboretum.

Mapping and labeling are an important part of the work done at Arnold. Along with being a horticultural garden, the arboretum is also a research facility. Visitors from many countries use the collections for study purposes, so maps showing where each individual specimen is located have been kept for more than seventy years.

Kelley was heavily involved in the arboretum's switch from hand-drawn maps to a computerized mapping system. Her role in this huge project was to transcribe the hand-drawn maps to the computerized versions and also to maintain current hand-drawn maps until the new system was completed.

There are two major plantings each year, in the spring and fall, when about a thousand new plants are added to the grounds. It is Kelley's responsibility to put all of these new plantings on the maps. She makes sure that every plant is labeled, a procedure that involves hanging two labels directly on the plant to provide an accession number, the name of the plant, the family, where it came from, and its map location.

Kelley's work with a plant begins when it goes from the nursery to the grounds. She prepares the labels, which are the size of credit cards and made of aluminum, by embossing the required information from the arboretum's database onto the labels, which she then attaches to the plants.

Kelley also performs field checks of each individual specimen to determine its condition. She recommends replacement of damaged or unhealthy plants to the horticultural taxonomist and informs the propagator if a specimen needs to be repropagated.

Most of Kelley's time is spent outdoors, even in winter, when much of the mapping and record keeping is done. It's the best time to field check the conifer collection of pines, firs, and spruce. It's also easier to find labels when there aren't any leaves on the trees, because the labels are hung above ground level.

Pluses and Minuses

Working outside is one of the things Kelley likes most about the job. "What I love most is being outdoors in this great collection of plants," she says. "It's one of the best collections in the world. There are very old specimens, and then we have all these new plants coming in. I also like that I have some indoor work. The computer work I do is challenging mentally. The mix is ideal."

The only stress Kelley experiences on her job comes from the fact that her department is understaffed. She says, "My job is extensive enough that three people should really be doing it." She does have volunteers and two summer interns to help, but training them is time-consuming and adds to her workload.

Kelley has a way to handle occasional stress, however. "Whenever I need to regroup, I can just go outside," she says. "I have a beautiful place in which to do it."

The Career Ladder for Mappers and Labelers

Kelley enjoys her job and feels that she could stay with it for a long time because there's so much to learn. With more experience and study, and after publishing some research results, it could be possible for a mapper and labeler to move up to a curatorial position.

Outreach Horticulturist, Arnold Arboretum

The mission of the Arnold Arboretum includes the goals of continuing research, education, and community outreach work.

Chris Strand works at the arboretum as an outreach horticulturist. He earned a bachelor's degree in biology from the University of Colorado in Boulder, concentrating on taxonomy, the study of the different species and how they are classified. After graduation Strand won a fellowship sponsored by Longwood Gardens and earned his master's degree in public horticulture at the University of Delaware in Newark. He worked for one year at Callaway Gardens near Atlanta, Georgia, before coming to the Arnold Arboretum.

Job Description

Strand is in charge of visitor services, a position with a wide range of duties. He develops and manages the exhibits that are shown in the exhibit hall, where information is passed on to visitors through an information desk, a photographic display, and a bookstore.

Strand trains the volunteers who are stationed in the hall to answer visitors' questions. He ascertains that the bookstore buyer has everything needed for the exhibit and makes sure there are maps of the grounds available so visitors can find their way around the grounds.

Strand also teaches in the adult education program. He covers woody plant identification and teaches a six-week course on the highlights of the arboretum. He describes his students as people with varied interests in continuing education; they include retired people, volunteers wanting to learn more about the plants, or rangers from the National Park Service. (The Arnold Arboretum maintains a cooperative arrangement with the National Park Service through which interpretive rangers are taught to conduct historical landscape restoration and maintenance.)

He also works with a consultant on an ongoing project to improve signage on the grounds. In addition, he answers requests for information about the arboretum and requests for publications. Strand supervises volunteers who run a plant answer-line once a week, and he supplies them with the materials they need for the job.

The part of his job that Strand most enjoys is spending time among the collections. He says, "My boss has made it clear that I'm supposed to be very familiar with everything, so I spend a lot of time going outside looking at plants, photographing them, learning about them. We have well over eleven thousand different specimens on the grounds, and the best part is that I always have the opportunity to learn more about them."

What he likes least is dealing with difficult people. Strand observes that since the Arnold Arboretum is a public park and does not charge admission, people occasionally disregard the rules. Some bring unleashed dogs or take cuttings from the plants.

Climbing the Career Ladder in Public Horticulture

Graduate programs in public horticulture are directed toward people who are interested in working in education or administration. Strand plans to continue working in public horticulture, hoping to eventually be in charge of a public program at an arboretum or botanical garden. Wherever his career takes him, though, he hopes to always have direct contact with the plants because they are what he loves most about the job.

Senior Biologist, Arboretum of Los Angeles County

Jim Bauml is a senior biologist with the Arboretum of Los Angeles County in Arcadia, California, a facility under the management of the Department of Parks and Recreation. He earned his B.S. degree in botany from Texas A&M University, his M.S. in botany from Cornell University, and his Ph.D. in botany from Claremont Graduate University. He has been working in the field for nearly twenty years.

Bauml realized in junior high school that he wanted to work with living things, having become fascinated by plants after a friend challenged him to grow some x-rayed zinnia seeds. He began reading about horticulture and botany, and he was hooked at once.

He also traveled throughout Mexico with an amateur plant collector during the summers, where he fell in love with the exotic plants he collected and brought back to Texas. Bauml knew his master's thesis would eventually be based on those travels, about sorting out the classification of spider lilies.

His first job after graduate school was as botanist at the Huntington Botanical Gardens in San Marino, California. While there, he learned that the botanist at the county arboretum was planning to retire. Since the arboretum was nearby and the salary was much higher than what he was currently earning, he applied for the job.

Bauml was hired as a senior biologist with an M.S. in botany and three and a half years of experience at Huntington.

One of the things Bauml likes most about his job is the freedom it allows and the fact that every day is different. Since the arboretum is a public facility, the taxpayers of Los Angeles County have a large say in its operation. Consequently, Bauml handles many calls each day from the public and interacts with visitors who come by with plant identification questions, plant selection problems, science fair problems, and other botanical questions. He describes the horticultural information consultant and librarian as "the frontline public servants," who are best equipped to handle questions about diseases, pests, weed control, pruning, and fertilizing.

One of Bauml's job priorities is making and placing the name and number metal tags and the plastic display signs on the plants. Since he uses an engraving machine for the signs, he's able to do what it used to take several staff members to accomplish. He relies heavily on volunteers to help with plant mapping, the photo archives, the herbarium, nursery work, and computer data entry. For the mapping function, one volunteer prints out a current inventory for one of the arboretum's 200 × 200 grid units, laying tapes around the area and then taking inventory and measuring each plant to the nearest foot. New labels are ordered and are made by another volunteer, who also places them on the plants. There are usually four or five volunteers working with Bauml among the plants during one three-hour period each week.

When arboretum work is less pressing, Bauml works on developing a course in useful plants, ethnobotany, or one of any number of projects for which he has grant money. One such project is about natural dyes used by a group of Indians in Mexico; another is a study of an endangered cactus along the Texas/Mexico border.

Bauml's days are usually busy but not overly pressured. However, he has experienced extremely hectic times with several deadlines to meet, as when he was responsible for two educational exhibits with a very limited budget.

Upsides

What Bauml likes most about his job is the chance to share botanical information and the freedom to work on any number of plant-related projects, both indoors and outdoors. He appreciates the fact that he also gets to learn when he answers questions for people. He finds it very satisfying to put signs on the plants so visitors can better enjoy their time at the arboretum and hopefully appreciate the plants more. In addition, he likes having very capable coworkers such as the librarian and horticultural consultant.

Downsides

The part of the job that Bauml likes least is the fact that the administration doesn't provide the level of leadership and organization needed for the arboretum to reach its full potential. He isn't asked for his opinion or included in any discussions about setting goals or developing exhibits, collections, and programs, which makes him feel that he isn't part of a creative team.

In addition, Bauml has asked for but not received paid time to do botanical exploration and research. He feels that he'd be much happier if he had three or four weeks a year for these endeavors. On the other hand, he has been able to attend annual botanical garden meetings for several years, which is when he has direct contact with his peers from other gardens.

Salaries

Bauml earns more than $50,000 with generous benefits. A regular biologist would start at around $33,000 and make $41,000 after five regular step raises. During good times, there are cost-of-living raises, too. Also related is vacation time. "We start with ten days each year. This eventually goes up to twenty days," he says.

"There are also twelve sick days per year, and up to six of these can be used as 'personal sick' (really vacation) days. And, of course, there are national holidays. Also, here we have alternate schedules. I work four ten-hour days and get Fridays off."

Professional Advice

Bauml suggests that botanical garden work can be very satisfying if you really love plants. He feels that plant work is a good background for such a career, although most schools now are more concerned with DNA than with whole plants and their environments.

Botanical research isn't part of most jobs, and unless it's a specific part of the job description, you shouldn't expect to do it. If you want to work in research, Bauml suggests considering an academic position with summers off for fieldwork as well as sabbaticals. But expect fierce competition for these positions and high pressure to publish research results.

If you're considering botanical garden work, Bauml advises applying for summer internships at botanical gardens for at least two years. This will give you a better idea of what's involved in the work. But you should choose your internship wisely to be sure you find one that will give you exposure to the curatorial and botanical sides of the field.

Horticulturist, Missouri Botanical Garden

Susan Farrington is a horticulturist with the Missouri Botanical Garden in St. Louis. She earned a B.A. in history at Haverford College in Pennsylvania, followed later by horticulture classes at Longwood Gardens (Certificate of Merit in Ornamental Plants) and at Temple University, the Ambler, Pennsylvania, campus.

Farrington says that she didn't plan to pursue a career in horticulture and describes herself as a good student who lacked direction. After graduating from college, she took a job as a recreational counselor with emotionally disturbed children, working in a program where she'd been volunteering. She stayed in that field for three and a half years, working on gardening projects with her clients and enjoying gardening at home.

Since she'd always loved plants, Farrington decided to take a part-time job at a large garden center in the Philadelphia area. Because it was only part-time, there were very few requirements other than basic gardening knowledge and good personal relations. Garden centers are frequently looking for good seasonal help, and permanent opportunities can often follow. Within a month, she quit her counseling job and went to work full-time at the garden center. In time, she worked her way up to the position of greenhouse/annuals manager at another large garden center.

Working in retail horticulture was an excellent education in itself, since Farrington was asked questions all day long and had to learn the answers and learn how to explain the information to others. Still, she decided to return to school and took a number of horticulture classes. Farrington says, "Having had a fair bit of work experience before I took any classes made me appreciate much more what I learned: I had observed how plants behaved, and the classes taught me why they did what they did."

After eight years in retail horticulture, Farrington decided she wanted to work in a botanical garden. Since she didn't have a horticulture degree, she knew it might be hard to break into the field. She sent out résumés across the East Coast and as far as the Midwest. She was interviewed at several gardens and was most impressed by the Missouri Botanical Garden, so she decided to relocate there.

Although Farrington's job description requires a horticulture degree, her employer felt that she had the equivalent, based on her previous job experience, numerous horticulture courses, and a degree in another field.

Farrington is the horticulturist in charge of two conservatories at the botanical garden: the Temperate House and the Linnean House. Her job includes doing whatever is necessary to keep the two houses looking their best. She plants and prunes flowers and shrubs, waters the plants, and mulches the beds. She also weeds the beds, removes finished flowers, changes floral displays, and decides which flowers to use each season and what permanent plants to install.

A typical day starts with opening up both houses and ensuring that everything is presentable: Is the temperature setting right? Are the vents open? Is there any litter to remove? Then she usually waters plants and might work on a project with the volunteers, such as changing floral displays or pruning.

Pros and Cons

Farrington enjoys the combination of physical and mental activity and the variety that the job allows. She says, "I could never sit at a desk all day, but I like to spend a little bit of time doing mental tasks such as designing plantings, ordering plants, or researching interpretive signs. I like the variety the most; I need to have my hands in the dirt, yet I also enjoy the mental challenges."

She describes the work atmosphere as considerably more relaxed than retail horticulture, which was very fast-paced and could be quite stressful. It's also rewarding when visitors appreciate and admire the gardens. In winter, Farrington likes working in the conservatory, when she can be surrounded by blooming plants despite the winter weather.

Farrington says that the physical work required for the job is both a positive and a negative. On the positive side, it keeps her in shape. On the negative, she worries about how many years she'll be able to do it.

She's also happy to be indoor horticulturist, which means that she doesn't have to participate in snow removal during the winter. In summer, the heat is a drawback. St. Louis experiences some extreme heat, and horticulturists seldom work in air-conditioning.

The other major downside for Farrington is salary because public horticulture is not a high-paying field. She took a large pay cut when she left retail horticulture, but she loves her work and is willing to make the sacrifice.

Professional Advice

Based on her experience, Farrington has some advice for aspiring horticulturists. "Don't invest a lot in a horticulture education until you have some good solid work experience," she suggests. "Make sure you really enjoy it and can handle the physical demands of the profession."

She recommends volunteering at a botanical garden as a way to gain valuable experience that can lead to employment opportunities. She also feels that working in retail horticulture for even a few months will provide you with a good background in the field. Farrington sums up her advice by saying, "You should love plants and gardening, you should be reasonably physically fit, and you better not mind getting dirty."

Appendix A

Professional Associations

THE FOLLOWING LIST can be used as a resource in locating information about specific careers. Many of the organizations publish newsletters listing job and internship opportunities, and others offer an employment service to members. A quick look at the organizations' names will give you an idea of their scope.

Landscape Architecture

The American Society of Landscape Architects is the professional group for landscape architects. Joining and becoming involved in projects sponsored by this nonprofit group will go a long way to nurture your career.

Additional information, including a list of colleges and universities offering accredited programs in landscape architecture, is available from:

American Society of Landscape Architects
636 Eye St. NW
Washington, DC 20001-3736
www.asla.org

For career information, contact:

American Nursery and Landscape Association
1000 Vermont Ave. NW, Ste. 300
Washington, DC 20005-2414
www.anla.org

American Society of Consulting Arborists
15245 Shady Grove Rd., Ste. 130
Rockville, MD 20850
www.asca-consultants.org

Canadian Society of Landscape Architects
P.O. Box 13594
Ottawa, ON K2K 1X6
www.csla.ca

PLANET (Professional Landcare Network)
950 Herndon Pkwy., Ste. 450
Herndon, VA 20170
www.landcarenetwork.org

Women in Landscape Architecture
American Society of Landscape Architects
636 Eye St. NW
Washington, DC 20001-3736
http://host.asla.org/groups/wlapigroup

General information on registration or licensing requirements is available from:

Council of Landscape Architectural Registration Boards (CLARB)
144 Church St., Ste. 201
Vienna, VA 22180
www.clarb.org

Urban and Regional Planning

Information on careers, salaries, and certification in urban and regional planning is available from:

American Planning Association
122 S. Michigan Ave., Ste. 1600
Chicago, IL 60603
www.planning.org

Canadian Institute of Planners
116 Albert St.
Ottawa, ON K1P 5G3
www.cip-icu.ca

Urban Land Institute
1025 Thomas Jefferson St. NW, Ste. 500 West
Washington, DC 20007
www.uli.org

Forestry, Range Management, and Conservation

For information about the forestry profession and lists of schools offering education in forestry, send a self-addressed, stamped business envelope to:

American Forest Foundation
1111 19th St. NW, Ste. 780
Washington, DC 20036
www.affoundation.org

American Forests
P.O. Box 2000
Washington, DC 20013
www.americanforests.org

Bureau of Land Management
U.S. Department of the Interior
1849 C St. NW, Rm. 3619
Washington, DC 20240
www.blm.gov

Canadian Forestry Association
203–185 Somerset St. West
Ottawa, ON K2P 0J2
www.canadianforestry.com

Canadian Institute of Forestry
504–151 Slater St.
Ottawa, ON K1P 5H3
www.cif-ifc.org

National Park Service
U.S. Department of the Interior
1849 C St. NW
Washington, DC 20240
www.nps.gov

National Wildlife Federation
11100 Wildlife Center Dr.
Reston, VA 20190-5362
www.nwf.org

Parks Canada
National Office
25 Eddy St.
Gatineau, QC K1A 0M5
www.parkscanada.ca

Society of American Foresters
5400 Grosvenor La.
Bethesda, MD 20814-2198
www.safnet.org

Society for Range Management
10039 W. 27th Ave.
Wheat Ridge, CO 80215-6601
www.rangelands.org

Soil and Water Conservation Society
945 SW Ankeny Rd.
Ankeny, IA 50023-9723
www.swcs.org

Student Conservation Association
1800 N. Kent St., Ste. 102
Arlington, VA 22209
www.thesca.org

U.S. Forest Service
U.S. Department of Agriculture
1400 Independence Ave. SW
Washington, DC 20250-0003
www.fs.fed.us

World Forestry Center
4033 SW Canyon Rd.
Portland, OR 97221
www.worldforestrycenter.org

Landscape Design

Association of Professional Landscape Designers
4305 N. 6th St., Ste. A
Hamburg, PA 17110
www.apld.com

Groundskeeping

The National Pest Management Association
9300 Lee Hwy., Ste. 301
Fairfax, VA 22031
www.pestworld.org

Professional Grounds Management Society
720 Light St.
Baltimore, MD 21230-3816
www.pgms.org

Golf Courses

Canadian Golf Superintendents Association
5520 Explorer Dr., Ste. 205
Mississauga, ON L4W 5L1
www.golfsupers.com

Golf Course Superintendents Association of America
1421 Research Park Dr.
Lawrence, KS 66049-3859
www.gcsaa.org

Cooperative Extension Service

Agriculture and Agri-Food Canada
Public Information Request Service
Sir John Carling Bldg.
930 Carling Ave.
Ottawa, ON K1A 0C5
www.agr.gc.ca

Cooperative State Research, Education, and Extension Service
(CSREES)
Waterfront Centre
800 Ninth St. SW
Washington, DC 20024
www.csrees.usda.gov

Botanical Gardens and Arboreta

The American Public Gardens Association (formerly the American
Association of Botanical Gardens and Arboreta) is the professional
association for public gardens in North America, supporting the
public horticulture community in its mission to study, display, and
conserve plants.

American Horticultural Society
7931 E. Boulevard Dr.
Alexandria, VA 22308
www.ahs.org

American Phytopathological Society
3304 Pilot Knob Rd.
St. Paul, MN 55121
www.apsnet.org

American Public Gardens Association
100 W. 10th St., Ste. 614
Wilmington, DE 19801
www.publicgardens.org

American Society of Consulting Arborists
15245 Shady Grove Rd., Ste. 130
Rockville, MD 20850
www.asca-consultants.org

Canadian Botanical Association
Box 160
Aberdeen, SK S0K 0A0
www.cba-abc.ca

Canadian Botanical Conservation Network
P.O. Box 399
Hamilton, ON L8N 3H8
www.rbg.ca/cbcn

International Society of Arboriculture
1400 W. Anthony Dr.
Champaign, IL 61821
www.isa-arbor.com

National Arbor Day Foundation/Institute
100 Arbor Ave.
Nebraska City, NE 68410
www.arborday.org

Tree Care Industry Association
3 Perimeter Rd., Unit 1
Manchester, NH 03103
www.treecareindustry.org

Selected List of Botanical Gardens and Arboreta

MOST BOTANICAL GARDENS and arboreta offer opportunities for plant lovers to gain hands-on experience through student internships, summer employment, and volunteer programs. The American Public Gardens Association (APGA) publishes a directory of more than five hundred programs at 125 institutions throughout the country. Information about ordering this directory is listed in the Additional Resources.

Following are selected lists of gardens in both the United States and Canada that you can contact on your own.

Arboretum of the Barnes Foundation
300 N. Latches La.
Merion, PA 19066
www.barnesfoundation.org/ed_a_garden

The Arboretum at Flagstaff
4001 S. Woody Mountain Rd.
Flagstaff, AZ 86001-8775
www.thearb.org

Arnold Arboretum of Harvard University
125 Arbor Way
Jamaica Plain, MA 02130-3500
www.arboretum.harvard.edu

Atlanta Botanical Garden
1345 Piedmont Ave. NE
Atlanta, GA 30309
www.atlantabotanicalgarden.org

Bartlett Arboretum
University of Connecticut
151 Brookdale Rd.
Stamford, CT 06903-4199
http://bartlett.arboretum.uconn.edu

Bayou Bend Gardens
1 Westcott
Houston, TX 77024
www.riveroaksgardenclub.org

Berkshire Botanical Garden
P.O. Box 826
Stockbridge, MA 01262
www.berkshirebotanical.org

Bernheim Arboretum and Research Forest
State Highway 245
P.O. Box 130
Clermont, KY 40110
www.bernheim.org

The Berry Botanic Garden
11505 SW Summerville Ave.
Portland, OR 97219
www.berrybot.org

Betty Ford Alpine Gardens
183 Gore Creek Dr.
Vail, CO 81657
www.bettyfordalpinegardens.org

Bickelhaupt Arboretum
340 S. 14th St.
Clinton, IA 52732-5432
www.bickarb.org

Blithewold Mansion, Gardens, and Arboretum
101 Ferry Rd. (Route 114)
Bristol, RI 02809
www.blithewold.org

Boerner Botanical Gardens
9400 Boerner Dr.
Hales Comers, WI 53130
www.boernerbotanicalgardens.org

Botanical Gardens and Arboreta in the United States
Alaska Botanical Garden
P.O. Box 202202
Anchorage, AK 99520
www.alaskabg.org

Brookgreen Gardens
1931 Brookgreen Dr.
Murrells Inlet, SC 29576
www.brookgreen.com

Brooklyn Botanic Garden
1000 Washington Ave.
Brooklyn, NY 11225
www.bbg.org

Cape Fear Botanical Garden
536 N. Eastern Blvd.
Fayetteville, NC 28301
www.capefearbg.org

Cheekwood Botanical Gardens
1200 Forrest Park Dr.
Nashville, TN 37205
www.cheekwood.org

Cheyenne Botanic Garden
710 S. Lion Parks Dr.
Cheyenne, WY 82001
www.botanic.org

Chicago Botanic Garden
1000 Lake Cook Rd.
Glencoe, IL 60022
www.chicagobotanic.org

Donald E. Davis Arboretum
Garden Dr. and College St.
Auburn, AL 36849-5407
www.auburn.edu/arboretum

Dyck Arboretum of the Plains
177 W. Hickory St.
Box 3000
Hesston, KS 67062
www.dyckarboretum.org

Flamingo Gardens
3750 Flamingo Rd.
Davie, FL 33330-1614
www.flamingogardens.org

Fullerton Arboretum
1900 Associated Rd.
Fullerton, CA 92831
http://arboretum.fullerton.edu

Green Spring Gardens Park
4603 Green Spring Rd.
Alexandria, VA 22312
www.fairfaxcounty.gov/parks/gsgp

Greenwell Ethnobotanical Garden
82-6188 Mamalahoa Hwy.
Captain Cook, HI 96704
www.bishopmuseum.org/exhibits/greenwell/greenwell

Hayes Arboretum
801 Elks Rd.
Richmond, IN 47374
www.hayesarboretum.org

Historic London Town and Gardens
839 Londontown Rd.
Edgewater, MD 21037
www.historiclondontown.com

Idaho Botanical Garden
2355 N. Penitentiary Rd.
Boise, ID 83712
www.idahobotanicalgarden.org

Inniswood Metro Gardens
940 Hempstead Rd.
Westerville, OH 43081
www.inniswood.org

Jungle Gardens
Highway 329 at Game Farm Rd.
Avery Island, LA 70513
http://members.cox.net/mryfon/avery.htm

Lakewold Gardens
12317 Gravelly Lake Dr.
Lakewood, WA 98499
www.lakewold.org

Lincoln Children's Zoo & Botanical Gardens
1222 S. 27th St.
Lincoln, NE 68502
www.lincolnzoo.org

Longwood Gardens
Route 1
P.O. Box 501
Kennett Square, PA 19348-0501
www.longwoodgardens.org

McCrory Gardens
South Dakota State University
6th St. and 22nd Ave.
Brookings, SD
www3.sdstate.edu/academics/collegeofagricultureand
    biologicalsciences

Medford Leas
1 Medford Leas Way
Medford, NJ 08055
www.medfordleas.org

Missouri Botanical Garden
4344 Shaw Blvd.
St. Louis, MO 63110
www.mobot.org

Mt. Cuba Center
P.O. Box 3570
Greenville, DE 19807-0570
www.mtcubacenter.org

Myriad Botanical Gardens
301 W. Reno
Oklahoma City, OK 73102
www.myriadgardens.com

New York Botanical Garden
Bronx River Pkwy. at Fordham Rd.
Bronx, NY 10458
www.nybg.org

Northland Arboretum
14250 Conservation Dr.
Brainerd, MN 56401
http://arb.brainerd.com

Pine Tree State Arboretum
153 Hospital St.
P.O. Box 344
Augusta, ME 04332
www.pinetreestatearboretum.org

Red Butte Garden and Arboretum
University of Utah
300 Wakara Way
Salt Lake City, UT 84108
www.redbuttegarden.org

Wilbur D. May Arboretum and Botanical Garden
Rancho San Rafael Regional Park
1595 N. Sierra
Reno, NV 89503
www.maycenter.com

Botanical Gardens and Arboreta in Canada

Butchard Gardens
Vancouver Island
800 Benvenuto Ave.
Brentwood Bay, BC V8M 1J8
www.butchartgardens.com

Calgary Zoo, Botanical Garden, and Prehistoric Park
1300 Zoo Rd. NE
Calgary, AB T23 7V6
www.calgaryzoo.org

Devonian Botanic Garden
University of Alberta
Edmonton, AB T6G 2E1
www.devonian.ualberta.ca

Harriet Irving Botanical Gardens
Acadia University
32 University Ave.
Wolfville, NS B4P 2R6
http://botanicalgardens.acadiau.ca

International Peace Garden
P.O. Box 419
Boissevain, MB R0K 0E0
www.peacegarden.com

Montreal Botanical Garden
4101 Sherbrooke East
Montreal, QC H1X 2B2
www2.ville.montreal.qc.ca/jardin/en

Niagara Parks Botanical Gardens
2565 Niagara Pkwy.
Niagara Falls, ON L2E 6T2
www.niagaraparks.com/nature/botanical.php

Nikka Yuko Japanese Garden
P.O. Box 751
Lethbridge, AB T1J 3Z6
www.japanesegarden.ab.ca

Oxen Pond Botanical Garden
Memorial University
St. John's, NF A1C 5S7
www.cdli.ca/vsc/botgard.html

Queen Elizabeth Park
4600 Cambie St.
Vancouver, BC V6G 1Z4
www.city.vancouver.bc.ca/parks/parks/queenelizabeth/index.htm

Royal Botanical Gardens
680 Plains Rd. West
Hamilton/Burlington, ON L7T 4H4
www.rbg.ca

UBC Botanical Garden
6804 SW Marine Dr.
Vancouver, BC V6T 1Z4
www.ubcbotanicalgarden.org

Van Dusen Botanical Garden
5251 Oak St.
Vancouver, BC V6M 4H1
www.vandusengarden.org

ADDITIONAL RESOURCES

THERE ARE MANY publications you can turn to for additional information about careers in landscape design, botanical gardens, and arboreta. The following are some examples to get you started.

APGA Publications

The following are publications of the American Public Gardens Association (APGA) and can be ordered directly by contacting:

American Public Gardens Association
100 W. 10th St., Ste. 614
Wilmington, DE 19801
www.publicgardens.org

Internship Directory. Lists more than five hundred summer jobs
and internships at 125 botanical gardens, arboreta, and other
horticultural institutions. Includes positions in grounds
management, education, collections, curation, and more.

The Public Garden. A quarterly journal. Each themed issue focuses
on topics of interest to public horticulture professionals.

Salary Survey. Contains the latest salary and benefit information
for twenty-two positions in administration, horticulture, and
education at U.S. and Canadian botanical gardens.

Magazines

Country Gardens. Contains color photographs, easy-to-follow
planting diagrams, and helpful advice for many garden
designs.

Fine Gardening. Gives hands-on advice, information, and
inspiration on garden design; intriguing plants; reliable
techniques; and practical landscaping projects.

Horticulture. Provides articles on gardening techniques, soil and
fertilizers, tools and equipment, greenhouses, seeds, nursery
stock, and pest and plant disease control.

House and Garden. Covers residential interior design and gardens.

Landscape Architecture. Is directed toward the professional
landscape architect; the main focus is on common problems of
developers and builders.

Landscape Management. Contains news and analysis of green
industry issues and regulations, equipment availability and
care, application and handling of control products,
ornamental installation and care, turfseed, business and
management practices, and new products.

Books

Amidon, Jane. *Moving Horizons: The Landscape Architecture of Kathryn Gustafson and Partners.* New York: Birlhauser, 2005.

Amidon, Jane. *Radical Landscapes: Reinventing Outdoor Space.* London: Thames and Hudson, 2004.

Bahamon, Alejandro. *Ultimate Landscape Design.* Kempen, Germany: Neues Publishing, 2006.

Bell, Simon. *Elements of Visual Design in the Landscape,* 2nd ed. London: Spon Press, 2004.

Berke, Philip R. *Urban Land Use Planning,* 5th ed. Champaign, Ill.: University of Illinois Press, 2006.

Blaisse, Petra. *Petra Blaisse Inside Outside: Interior and Landscape Architecture.* Rotterdam, Netherlands: NAI Publishers, 2006.

Booth, Norman K., and James E. Hiss. *Residential Landscape Architecture: Design Process for the Private Residence,* 4th ed. Upper Saddle River, N.J.: Prentice Hall, 2004.

Camenson, Blythe. *Careers for Plant Lovers and Other Green-Thumb Types,* 2nd ed. Chicago: McGraw-Hill, 2004.

Christensen, Alan. *Dictionary of Landscape Architecture and Construction.* New York: McGraw-Hill, 2005.

Curl, James S. *A Dictionary of Architecture and Landscape Architecture,* 2nd ed. New York: Oxford University Press, 2006.

Garner, Jerry. *Careers in Horticulture and Botany,* 2nd ed. Chicago: McGraw-Hill, 2006.

Links International, ed. *Landscape Design Today.* Corte Madera, Calif.: Gingko Press, 2004.

Mostafavi, Mohsen, and Ciro Najle. *Landscape Urbanism: A Manual for the Machinic Landscape.* London: Architectural Association Publications, 2004.

Murphy, Michael D. *Landscape Architecture Theory: An Evolving Body of Thought.* Long Grove, Ill.: Waveland Press, 2005.

Preece, John E., and Paul E. Read. *The Biology of Horticulture: An Introductory Textbook,* 2nd ed. New York: John Wiley and Sons, 2005.

Reed, Peter. *Groundswell: Constructing the Contemporary Landscape.* New York: Museum of Modern Art, 2005.

Saunders, William S. *Urban Planning Today.* Minneapolis: University of Minnesota Press, 2006.

Steenbergen, Clemens, and Wouter Reh. *Architecture and Landscape: The Design Experiment of the Great European Gardens and Landscapes.* New York: Birlhauser, 2004.

Theokas, Andrew. *Grounds for Review: The Garden Festival in Urban Planning and Design.* Liverpool: Liverpool University Press, 2005.

Trieb, Marc. *Settings and Stray Paths: Writings on Landscape Architecture.* Abingdon, UK: Taylor and Francis, 2005.

Walker, Peter. *Peter Walker and Partners Landscape Architecture: Defining the Craft.* Oxford: ORO Editions, 2005.

About the Author

A FULL-TIME WRITER of career books, Blythe Camenson's main concern is helping job seekers make educated choices. She firmly believes that readers can find long-term, satisfying careers with enough information. To that end, she researches traditional as well as unusual occupations, talking to a variety of professionals about what their jobs are really like. In all of her books, she includes first-hand accounts from people who can reveal what to expect in each occupation.

Camenson was educated in Boston, earning her B.A. in English and psychology from the University of Massachusetts and her M.Ed. in counseling from Northeastern University.

In addition to *Opportunities in Landscape Architecture, Botanical Gardens, and Arboreta,* she has written more than thirty books for McGraw-Hill.